First published in 2006 by New Holland Publishers (UK) Ltd
London • Cape Town • Sydney • Auckland
Garfield House, 86–88 Edgware Road, London W2 2EA, United Kingdom
www.newhollandpublishers.com
80 McKenzie Street, Cape Town 8001, South Africa
14 Aquatic Drive, Frenchs Forest, NSW 2086, Australia
218 Lake Road, Northcote, Auckland

Copyright © 2006 text AG&G Books
The right of David Squire to be identified as author of this work has been asserted by him in accordance with the Copyright, Designs and Patents Act 1988.
Copyright © 2006 illustrations and photographs New Holland Publishers (UK) Ltd
Copyright © 2006 New Holland Publishers (UK) Ltd

ISBN 1 84537 107 0
10 9 8 7 6 5 4 3 2 1

Editorial Direction: Rosemary Wilkinson Senior Editor: Clare Hubbard Production: Hazel Kirkman
Designed and created for New Holland by AG&G Books Copyright © 2004 "Specialist" AG&G Books
Design: Glyn Bridgewater Illustrations: Dawn Brend, Gill Bridgewater and Ann Winterbotham
Editor: Alison Copland Photographs: see page 80
Reproduction by Pica Digital Pte Ltd, Singapore
Printed and bound in Malaysia by Times Offset (M) Sdn. Bhd.

The information in this book is true and complete to the best of our knowledge. All recommendations are made without guarantee on the part of the authors and the publishers. The authors and publishers disclaim any liability for damages or injury resulting from the use of this information.

The HERB GARDEN

Specialist

The essential guide to growing herbs and designing, planting, improving and caring for herb gardens

David Squire

Series editors: A. & G. Bridgewater

NEW HOLLAND

Contents

Author's foreword **2**

Author's foreword

Culinary herbs are some of the oldest and best-known plants, and in medieval times they were used to cloak incipient decay in food, as well as adding interesting flavours to meals that otherwise might have been dull and monotonous. Culinary herbs are still widely used and many offer distinctive flavours; others are added as a garnish to salads, sandwiches and other dishes.

Medicinal herbs are also popular, and in earlier times these were the prime source of remedies. Books known as Herbals were popular, and one of the most widely known is Nicholas Culpeper's *English Physitian*, first published in 1652 and later referred to as his *Herbal*; it offered remedies developed and used in his own medical practice.

Today, culinary herbs are popular in gardens of all sizes and shapes. Many can also be grown in containers on patios, or on balconies and windowsills. This highly illustrated and practical book describes a wide range of herbs, from Chives to Ginger. Most of them are ideal for growing in temperate climates, while a few are less hardy and need protection in winter. The book covers methods of harvesting, storing and using herbs, as well as looking after and raising your own plants, whether from seeds, cuttings or division. Many herbs are also ideal for use in nosegay gardens, flower arrangements and pot-pourri. This book will enrich your garden with plants, as well as adding distinctive flavours to your food.

SEASONS

Throughout this book, advice is given about the best times to look after plants. Because of global and even regional variations in climate and temperature, the four main seasons have been used, with each subdivided into 'early', 'mid-' and 'late' – for example, early spring, mid-spring and late spring. These 12 divisions of the year can be converted into the appropriate calendar months in your local area, if you find this helps.

Measurements

Both metric and imperial measurements are given in this book – for example, 1.8 m (6 ft).

Warning

Pregnant women should consult a doctor before consuming any herbs or herbal teas.

What are herbs?

Most herbs are easy to grow in borders, where they can be mixed with ornamental plants, in beds entirely devoted to them, in cartwheel herb gardens, in draughtboard designs, and in windowboxes and decorative herb pots. They can also be grown in pots and troughs on balconies. By far the majority of these herbs are hardy and some, such as Mints, grow from year to year until they are congested and the clumps need to be lifted and divided.

Are they difficult to grow?

POPULAR HERBS

Although there are many culinary herbs, six of them (see below) are especially popular. There are others, too, and they all play a role in adding flavour to food and drinks, as well as being used as garnishes.

Chives

- **Chives:** bulbous, with tubular, onion-flavoured leaves (see page 28).

Mint

- **Mint:** several kinds, but the best-known one is Spearmint (see page 46).

Parsley

- **Parsley:** popular for garnishing dishes, as well as adding to sauces (see page 54).

Sage

- **Sage:** grey-green, wrinkled leaves, used fresh or dried and added to food such as rich meat and poultry; also used in stuffings (see page 59).

Tarragon

- **Tarragon:** leaves used to flavour meat and fish, as well as adding to omelettes (see page 35).

Thyme

- **Thyme:** well known for its leaves which are used to flavour food (see page 64).

Above: Several herbs are ideal for growing in containers such as windowboxes or troughs. Even tall herbs, while they are still small, can be planted in them.
Right: Stone sinks, securely raised on bricks to allow for good drainage, can be used for growing many distinctive herbs.

Growing cycles of herbs

These are diverse and reflect the wide range of garden plants. They include:

- **Annuals:** single-season plants – sowing, flowering and dying within the same year.
- **Biennials:** these have a two-year growing and flowering cycle.
- **Bulbs:** these are swollen bases, formed of fleshy, modified leaves tightly packed around each other.
- **Herbaceous perennials:** these long-term plants die down to soil level in autumn and send up fresh shoots in spring.
- **Shrub-like:** these have a woody structure and the ability to live for many years. Some are hardy, while others are slightly tender and in temperate climates may lose some or all of their leaves. Some shrubs are deciduous and others evergreen.

WHICH PARTS OF HERBS TO USE

Herbs are grown for their leaves, flowers, seeds, stems and bulbs. The A–Z of culinary herbs (pages 26–65) describes the parts that are used.

Culinary or medicinal?

What is the difference?

Culinary herbs are used in cooking. Many are prized for their aromatic leaves; others produce spicy seeds, stems that can be candied, or bulbs with a distinctive aroma. A few, such as Horseradish and Liquorice, have roots that yield strong, pungent and distinctive flavours. Medicinal herbs are plants that for thousands of years have been used to relieve medical problems. Some herbs have both culinary and medicinal uses.

PLANT SIZES AND PARTS USED

Culinary herbs range both in size and in the parts used, from bulbs to seeds and leaves.

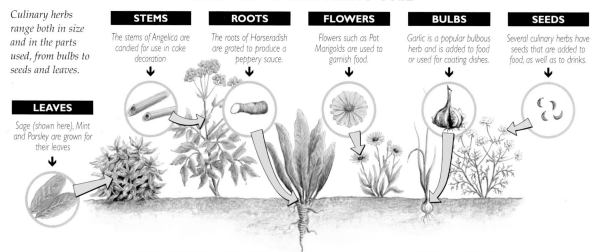

STEMS
The stems of Angelica are candied for use in cake decoration

ROOTS
The roots of Horseradish are grated to produce a peppery sauce.

FLOWERS
Flowers such as Pot Marigolds are used to garnish food.

BULBS
Garlic is a popular bulbous herb and is added to food or used for coating dishes.

SEEDS
Several culinary herbs have seeds that are added to food, as well as to drinks.

LEAVES
Sage (shown here), Mint and Parsley are grown for their leaves

CULINARY HERBS

Herbs used in cooking range in size from the ground-hugging evergreen and shrub-like Thyme to the dominant Angelica, a tall, hardy biennial which can also be grown as a short-term perennial. Some culinary herbs also have medicinal qualities; these include Angelica, Aniseed, Dill, Fennel, Parsley and Rosemary. Within this book, however, they are considered as culinary types, although pieces of historical information are given for many of the plants in the A–Z of culinary herbs (see pages 26–65).

MEDICINAL HERBS

Throughout the world there are plants with healing properties that are used in medical treatments. A few culinary herbs have medicinal qualities, while other plants are solely known for their curative powers. These include the well-known *Atropa bella-donna* (Belladonna; also known as Dwale and Deadly Nightshade), which yields the drug atropine used in the treatment of eye problems. It gains its common name from the Italian *bella*, meaning beautiful, and *donna* for lady; during the Renaissance, ladies used it to beautify and enlarge the pupils of their eyes.

Other plants do not have such a rich heritage, but nevertheless were greatly valued for their medicinal qualities. *Urtica dioica* (Stinging Nettle), a well-known wasteland and roadside plant, is thought to have been spread by the Roman legions in their conquest of Europe. Soldiers are said to have been unhappy with the cold, damp, northerly weather and rubbed their limbs with Nettle leaves to enliven their blood circulation. It also relieved rheumatism and toothache!

There are many other medicinal herbs, but within this book we concentrate on those used in cookery.

Flavours galore

Most aromas and flavours produced by herbs are strong and distinctive, as they have to impart themselves on food. A few are claimed to complement and draw out flavours in food. Yet, whatever the culinary explanation, they are distinctive.

Some herbs have achieved near cult status and, perhaps, Garlic is one of these. Controversially, some French cooks claim that it cloaks the natural flavour in food and is only used by inexperienced cooks, while others are enthusiastic about its use and generously add it to food as well as coating serving bowls with it.

In ancient Rome, as well as during Shakespeare's time in the sixteenth century, Garlic was claimed to be the aroma of vulgarity. However, it has several medicinal uses, especially in the treatment of asthma, coughs and hoarseness; it is also claimed to repel vampires!

Herbs in the kitchen

Herbs are used in many ways in the preparation and cooking of food, as well as garnishing dishes to give them greater eye appeal. The A–Z of culinary herbs (see pages 26–65) details a wide range of herbs, with suggestions of the ways in which they can be used and, where applicable, the food usually associated with them. Drying and freezing herbs (see pages 74–75) also makes them available throughout winter when fresh ones are not obtainable.

How are culinary herbs used?

SEASONING

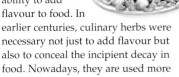

Herbs are best known for their ability to add flavour to food. In earlier centuries, culinary herbs were necessary not just to add flavour but also to conceal the incipient decay in food. Nowadays, they are used more reservedly and to complement food. Use them in moderation until their effect on food is known.

GARNISHING

Leaves, seeds and flowers are used to add visual appeal to food, although many also add flavour. The decorative appeal of flowers such as *Calendula officinalis* (Pot Marigold) is used to add colour to salads, while those of Borage are added to cold drinks, including claret cup, to give eye appeal and a refreshing flavour. However, be careful not to allow them to visually dominate food and drinks.

TEAS

Herbal teas, an infusion of one or more herbs, have been popular for their curative values for many years. Some involve culinary herbs such as Balm, Hyssop, Marjoram and Sage. Balm, for example, is used to make Balm tea, which is an especially refreshing drink when you are feeling ill. Longevity was another claim made for herbal infusions. When making them, use fresh, young leaves and avoid those damaged by pests and diseases.

What are 'mixed herbs'?

As the name suggests, these are mixtures of chopped herbs, used fresh or dried and usually with meat and fish dishes. The main herbs in these mixtures are Sage, Thyme, Marjoram and Parsley, although others are added according to taste.

Sage

Parsley

What are fines herbes?

This is a French term for finely chopped herbs, such as Chives, Parsley, Thyme and Tarragon. They are used fresh or dried, as seasonings and to flavour sauces. They are particularly associated with egg dishes.

Thyme

Chives

What is bouquet garni?

A bunch of herbs, tied together or wrapped in cheesecloth, used as a seasoning for food. The plural is *bouquets garnis*.

Marjoram

Tarragon

What are essential oils?

Volatile oils, each usually having the characteristic odour of the plant from which is it derived, used in perfumes and flavourings. They are frequently added to pot-pourri (see pages 24–25).

Herbs in pot-pourri

This is a way to create a rich range of fragrances indoors over a long period (see pages 24–25).

Herbs in flower arrangements

Many herbs are superb when cut and displayed in vases and other containers indoors (see pages 22–23).

Nosegays

Nowadays, nosegays are better known as bunches of attractive, fragrant flowers, or posies. Gardens in which the plants for this purpose were grown were known as nosegay gardens, and they were packed with stimulating and varied fragrances (see pages 20–21).

Herbs in gardens and containers

How do I grow culinary herbs?

There are many places in which herbs can be grown, from adding them to a medley of cottage-garden plants to planting in beds clinically cut into a lawn. Cartwheel herb gardens, draughtboard displays and groups of containers packed with herbs are other ways. If you like their cool and refreshing fragrances, you could also try a nosegay garden, or a small area set aside for those herbs that can be picked and displayed indoors.

GARDEN AND CONTAINER OPTIONS

Cartwheel herb gardens

↗ Few herb-garden features are as eye-catching as a cartwheel placed on its side on prepared soil and with low-growing herbs planted between the spokes. Even if a cartwheel is not available, the shape of a wheel can be simulated by stones to form the hub, spokes and rim. Further colour can be added – after plants have been put in position – by covering the soil with shingle.

Formal herb gardens

↗ These herb gardens are ideal where their surroundings also radiate formality. They have a regular shape and are ideal for fusing with a formal lawn. In shape, the garden can be square, oblong or round, but is usually sectioned into symmetrical parts. Small, low, evergreen hedges, perhaps formed of *Buxus sempervirens* 'Suffruticosa' (Dwarf Box), can be used to unite the herb garden.

Informal herb gardens

← These have a cottage-garden feel, with medleys of plants in informal arrangements. Herbs can be added, with tall and distinctive ones such as Angelica towards the back and diminutive ones along the front. Many herbs with umbrella-like seedheads, such as Dill, Fennel, Caraway and Chervil, have a relaxed habit and are ideal for mixing with border plants – but do not crowd them together.

GARDEN AND CONTAINER OPTIONS (CONTINUED)

Corner and narrow beds

↗ → Many modern gardens have only space for narrow borders, or perhaps a corner bed. Yet this need not be a problem, as the heights and spreads of herbs vary; by choosing suitable types, all spaces can be filled and a magnificent display created. Take care, however, not to use spreading types such as Mints, unless they are planted in bottomless pots.

Paved herb gardens

↘ These are open in nature, with paving slabs laid in patterns, perhaps in a draughtboard design or in rows, with herbs planted in gaps left between them. The firm, all-weather surface enables herbs to be reached throughout the year, whatever the weather. If you want to use a wheelbarrow or walking frame, choose a design with continuous rows of slabs. All-weather bricks can also be used in attractive patterns.

Herbs in containers

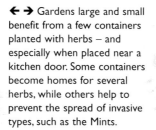

← → Gardens large and small benefit from a few containers planted with herbs – and especially when placed near a kitchen door. Some containers become homes for several herbs, while others help to prevent the spread of invasive types, such as the Mints.

Colour-designed herb gardens

→ Large herb gardens are superb when planted with colour-leaved herbs to create attractive patterns. These are often provided by colour-leaved forms of Sages (see page 19).

Cottage gardens

These, like informal gardens, have a relaxed character and encompass annuals, herbaceous perennials, shrubs, fruit trees and vegetables, as well as climbers as a background or, perhaps, clambering up tripods and old tree stumps.

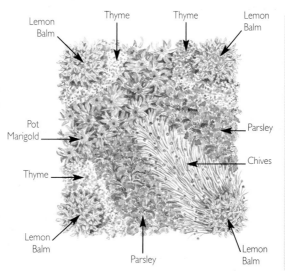

Lemon Balm
Thyme
Thyme
Lemon Balm
Pot Marigold
Parsley
Thyme
Chives
Lemon Balm
Parsley
Lemon Balm

NOSEGAY GARDENS

These are fragrant areas, partly planted with annuals and herbaceous plants as well as herbs with scented flowers and aromatic leaves (see page 20 for details of this unusual and exciting way to grow herbs).

Many of these fragrant plants can be used in flower arrangements.

Design and construction

**What are the
essentials?**

The more thorough the creation of the infrastructure for a herb garden, the longer it will remain in good condition. Poor, weak and shallow foundations soon cause paving slabs to settle and walls to crack and break, especially if the soil is mainly clay and likely to dry out in summer. Take your time in getting the basics right. Using the right tools will make construction easy – and remember that lifting heavy slabs is best tackled by two people.

PLANNING HARD LANDSCAPING

Detailed planning is essential if good results are to be achieved. Allow plenty of thinking and assessing time before deciding on the type of infrastructure and nature of the herb garden.

- Assess the site from a number of different viewpoints, both nearby and from inside house windows.
- Gain inspiration from specialist books and by visiting established herb gardens. Take along a notebook and measuring tape.
- Visit garden centres and builder's yards (merchants) to gain ideas of materials and their cost. Usually, manufacturers' brochures are free and these are good reminders of the shapes and sizes of paving and bricks, as well as other materials. Check on delivery costs.
- Carefully measure the area and draw it on scaled paper. Mark in positions for footings and paths. Make sure paths are wide enough for two people. Check the drainage from paved areas, so that rainwater quickly drains away.
- Transfer the plan to the construction area, using strings to mark footings and building lines.

Firm surfaces create ideal places for herbs grown in containers and grouped in clusters.

MATERIALS AND TOOLS

Materials

The range of materials for paths, edgings and walls is wide; some are relatively inexpensive, others ornate and costly. Choose materials that suit the style of the garden – formal or informal. Reconstituted stone pavers have an aged look, while ornate edgings introduce a Victorian ambience.

Sand   Cement   Ballast   Brick   Paver   Flat stone

Concrete paving slab   Reconstituted stone   Stone setts

Gravel   Border edging   Reconstituted stone edging and corner post

Log roll   Railway (railroad) sleeper

Tools

Before starting major construction work, check you have all the equipment you will need. Some are everyday gardening tools; others are specialized and essential for brickwork and foundations, including a builder's (carpenter's) spirit-level, club (stonemason's) hammer and trowels.

Tape measure   Pegs and string

Wheelbarrow   Spade   Shovel   Sledgehammer   Spirit-level

Garden rake

Pointing trowel (for finishing joints)

Bricklayer's (mason's) trowel

Club hammer   Bolster (brick) chisel   Line set (for bricklaying)

HOW TO BUILD WALLS

Building options

There are several important considerations.
- Wide, thick, level and strong foundations are essential.
- If a retaining wall, ensure water can escape from the soil-retained side. This involves using plenty of coarse drainage material, creating weeping holes through the wall, and ensuring that the wall is at least two bricks thick.
- If a high retaining wall, slightly angle it so that it slopes backwards from its base. This is known as a battered wall.
- If a single-brick wall and without piers, limit the height to 45 cm (18 in). With piers every 1.8 m (6 ft), increase the height to a maximum of 1.5 m (5 ft).
- If a double-brick wall and without piers, limit the height to 1.2 m (4 ft). With piers every 1.8 m (6 ft), increase the height to a maximum of 1.8 m (6 ft).

Dry-stone walls

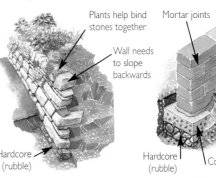

Plants help bind stones together

Wall needs to slope backwards

Hardcore (rubble)

↗ *Ensure that water can freely drain from soil behind the wall.*

Brick walls

Mortar joints

Hardcore (rubble)   Concrete

↗ *Strong foundations are essential; use mortar (see below) to lay bricks.*

HOW TO LAY PAVING

Paving options

There are several paving options – here are three.
- Concrete paving slabs need a firm base. For paths, a 5 cm (2 in) thick compacted hardcore (rubble) base, with a similar thickness of sharp sand, is sufficient. Lay slabs on top, using five blobs of mortar (see below for a suitable mixture).
- Wooden, slatted tiles, about 45 cm (18 in) square, have an informal appearance and, like concrete paving slabs, can be placed on a bed of sharp sand. Alternate the slabs so that their slats create an attractive pattern.
- Natural stone paving has an informal look, but is expensive. Lay each piece on sharp sand, with spaces between for prostrate plants to be planted.

Paving slabs

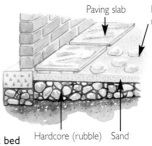

Paving slab   Blobs of mortar

Hardcore (rubble)   Sand

↑ *Lay paving slabs on five blobs of mortar. A firm, level base is essential.*

Crazy (cleft stone) paving

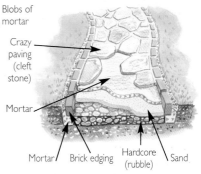

Crazy paving (cleft stone)

Mortar

Mortar   Brick edging   Hardcore (rubble)   Sand

↗ *Lay crazy paving (cleft stone) on a firm base: put large pieces at the edges, smaller pieces inside.*

Pavers and patterns for paving

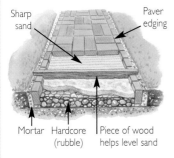

Sharp sand   Paver edging

Mortar   Hardcore (rubble)   Piece of wood helps level sand

↗ *Pavers are laid on a bed of sharp sand, with strong edges.*

Pavers can be laid in any one of several attractive patterns; some have a formal appearance, others informal.

Basket weave

Running stretcher

Running bond

Herringbone

Square pattern

Striped pattern

Mortar recipe for laying bricks and bedding slabs

1 part masonry cement and 5 of builder's sand. Usually, a plasticizer (to make the mixture more workable) has been added to the masonry cement. Alternatively, use 1 part Portland cement, 6 of builder's sand, and 1 of hydrated lime.

Cartwheel herb gardens

*Are these
suitable for
small
gardens?*

Because the herbs are constrained to a small, circular area, this is an ideal way to grow herbs in a restricted space. A wheel area about 1.8 m (6 ft) wide is ideal, especially if it is surrounded by a firm-surfaced, all-weather path. However, because each herb is constrained to a relatively small area, be prepared to lift, divide and replant every few years, as soon as they are congested. Most of these herbs are low-growing, although central and accent ones are taller.

PLANNING A CARTWHEEL DESIGN IN YOUR GARDEN

Integrating a cartwheel herb feature into a small garden can be a problem, but there are several inspirational ways to achieve this.

- Position the cartwheel design to one side of the garden and partly surrounded by a lawn; it then looks part of the overall design. Another option is to surround it with a crazy-paving (cleft-stone) path linked to the house by stepping stones.
- Position the cartwheel design in the centre of the garden and have a central path that

divides and encircles it before again proceeding down the garden. Two further paths, each radiating sideways from this central display, help to give further access.

- Integrate a cartwheel-type herb garden into a large patio. Ensure that the soil is well drained and that water from the patio area does not drain into the soil and cause waterlogging.

This cartwheel herb feature introduces a shape variation into a rectangular garden.

MAKING A ROUND HERB GARDEN

Even if a cartwheel is not available, or one cannot be simulated by the use of large pebbles, it is possible to create an attractive round herb garden. It can have the same radial structure of a wheel, with herbs clustered together in segments but without the clear demarcation created by spokes.

Herbs are planted in the same way as when in a cartwheel, but because there are no barriers between the groups of plants more vigilance is needed to ensure that neighbouring plants are not overwhelmed. Regular trimming is therefore needed, especially after a few years when the plants are growing strongly.

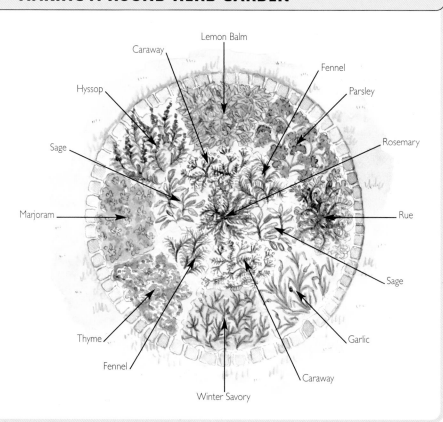

Caraway
Lemon Balm
Fennel
Hyssop
Parsley
Sage
Rosemary
Marjoram
Rue
Sage
Thyme
Garlic
Fennel
Caraway
Winter Savory

HOW TO MAKE A GARDEN WITH A CARTWHEEL

Few herb-garden features are as visually exciting as a cartwheel laid flat on the soil with herbs planted between the spokes. However, before preparing the soil and putting it in position, check that the wheel is strongly constructed and painted a bright colour that enables it to be seen even in twilight.

Prepare the soil by digging and removing perennial weeds. Then put the wheel in position and, if necessary, top up the soil between the spokes. Use small, healthy plants and, when planting is complete, gently but thoroughly water the area.

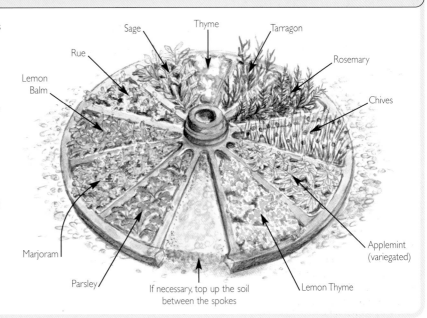

Sage Thyme Tarragon
Rue Rosemary
Lemon Balm Chives
Marjoram Applemint (variegated)
Parsley
If necessary, top up the soil between the spokes
Lemon Thyme

HOW TO MAKE A CARTWHEEL GARDEN USING LARGE PEBBLES

If it is not convenient to use a cartwheel, large pebbles can be used in place of the spokes and hub. By leaving a wide, round area at the hub, it becomes possible to plant a dominant, long-lived herb such as *Laurus nobilis* (Bay Laurel) in that position.

Where the areas are large, divide them with a row of pebbles, perhaps replicated and between other spokes. Try to create symmetry with the planting, especially if the wheel is in a formal area.

INSTEAD OF COBBLESTONES

• In rustic situations, use sticks to simulate the spokes.

• In formal areas, strips of wood, the length of the spoke and perhaps 10–15 cm (4–6 in) wide, can be pushed into the soil, leaving 5 cm (2 in) exposed.

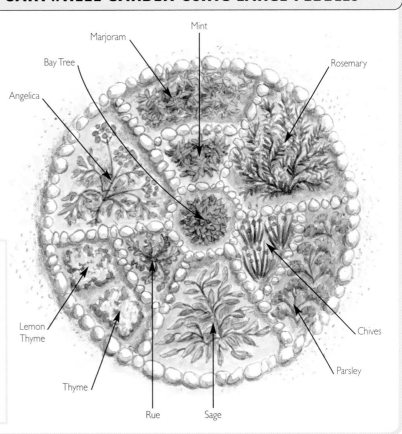

Marjoram Mint
Bay Tree Rosemary
Angelica
Lemon Thyme Chives
Thyme Parsley
Rue Sage

Paved herb gardens

What are their advantages?

Paved herb gardens have many advantages, including an all-weather surface, the ability to create attractive patterns, and the clinical separation of one herb from another to prevent their spread. Differently coloured but harmonizing slabs can be used to create further interest, but do not use garish colours. Paved herb gardens, perhaps with raised beds, are ideal for gardeners in wheelchairs, while some designs give easy access to wheelbarrows.

PLANNING A PAVED DESIGN IN YOUR GARDEN

This square herb garden creates a formal feature to one side of a garden.

Integrating a paved herb garden into a small garden is not difficult, especially if the garden is square or rectangular. Here are a few ways to create inspirational designs.

- Square and rectangular paved herb gardens are easily introduced into gardens with a similar shape. They have a formal nature, although if gravel can be introduced the design assumes slight informality.
- Paved herb gardens can be extensions of formal patios, and this enables easy care and harvesting. Raised herb gardens are also ideal features on patios.
- A framework of gravel paths edged in strong wood or ornamental edgings introduce informality, despite having a square or rectangular outline.
- Weathered brick paths create an aged ambience and are superb in rural areas and informal gardens. Ensure that they are well secured on a bed of sand constrained by strong edgings, or on concrete.
- Use coloured gravels to create extra colour, as well as highlighting and complementing these attractive plants.

Spaces left in patios and other paved areas are ideal as homes for culinary herbs. Plant Dwarf Box along the edges.

Draughtboard design

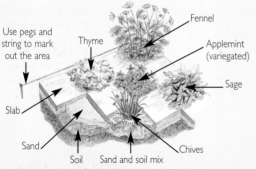

Use pegs and string to mark out the area

Thyme

Fennel

Applemint (variegated)

Sage

Slab

Sand

Soil

Sand and soil mix

Chives

In this design, square paving slabs are laid in a draughtboard-like arrangement, with the spaces used for herbs. There are two ways of creating these displays, depending on their permanency.

- Draughtboard displays are easily formed by laying slabs on a thin layer of sharp sand on flat, firm, well-prepared soil (ensure that the roots of perennial weeds have been removed).

- Integral, 'permanent' draughtboard displays on patios need strong foundations.

Raised herb gardens

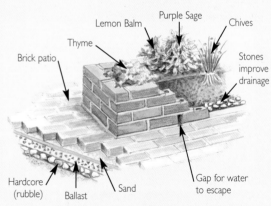

Lemon Balm

Purple Sage

Chives

Thyme

Brick patio

Stones improve drainage

Hardcore (rubble)

Ballast

Sand

Gap for water to escape

These are ideal for integrating with patios and other paved or brick surfaces. They can be constructed from bricks or wood, but make sure the compost is well drained and free from perennial weeds, and that excess water can escape through drainage holes left at the base.

MORE PAVED HERB-GARDEN DESIGNS

Bricks or paving blocks

↗ Small spaces, randomly left in brick or paving-block areas, create homes for herbs. Ensure that the bricks or paving blocks are laid in 'squared' patterns.

↗ Raised beds constructed of bricks are ideal for herbs. Use trailing types, with attractive flowers or leaves, to soften the edges and to make them more appealing.

Random and staggered paving slabs

↗ Paving slabs, in random as well as staggered patterns, can be laid on a thick base of sharp sand, with ground-hugging and bushy herbs planted between them.

Paving slabs

← Closely placed, randomly shaped and sized paving slabs with odd gaps have an informal appearance. Use low and ground-hugging herbs.

← Paving slabs, with equally spaced gaps between them and filled with shingle, create a formal look. Use ground-hugging herbs.

Wood construction

← Thick, rot-resistant planking can be used to construct a formal area for herbs, including tall, bushy and ground-hugging types.

← Rustic poles, held in place by vertical stakes, create an informal area for herbs, both when planted and still in their containers.

FILLING THE GAPS BETWEEN SLABS

Where gaps are not desired between closely positioned paving slabs, fill these with a cement and sand mixture.

About a week after laying paving slabs, fill the gaps between them by compressing a slightly moist mixture of 1 part cement and 3 parts sharp sand into them.

Do not allow this mixture to spread onto the surfaces of slabs, as it will stain them. Use masking tape along their edges to prevent staining.

Narrow, corner and 'island' beds

Can I grow herbs in 'awkward' places?

Narrow beds or borders are ideal places for growing small, relatively low-growing culinary herbs, because they allow easy access to the plants for weeding and other maintenance tasks, as well as for harvesting the leaves, flowers and seedheads. Corner beds are also good places for growing herbs, as are small rectangular or oval 'island' beds, perhaps cut into a lawn or surrounded by an all-weather path.

Attractive, firm-surfaced paths allow all-weather access to herbs throughout the year.

PLANNING HERB BORDERS FOR SMALL GARDENS

Invariably, new herb beds when fitted into an existing garden have to adapt to an earlier overall design, but this need not be a problem. Whether round and in the style of a cartwheel (see pages 10–11), or corner-shaped, narrow, small and rectangular or oval, all offer opportunities for growing culinary herbs.

Both low and medium-height herbs can be used to cloak the edges of paths.

NARROW AND OVAL HERB BORDERS

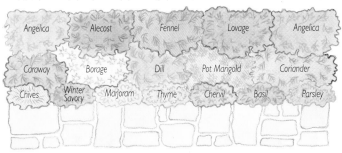

Narrow borders fronted by a firm-surfaced path and backed by a wall create sheltered places for growing herbs. Leave a 30–45 cm (12–18 in) gap between the herbs and the wall.

An oval bed, perhaps cut into a lawn, is always distinctive. Slightly mounding the bed in the middle makes central plants easier to see.

CORNER AND RECTANGULAR HERB BORDERS

Below: Corner beds, whether they are nestling between a wall and path or alongside a lawn, can often be very attractive features.
Right: A large rectangular bed will benefit from a firm-surfaced path running all the way around it, to make the plants more accessible.

Cottage herb gardens

Herbs are natural components of cottage gardens, where they mingle with flowers, fruit trees and bushes, and vegetables. These mixed borders are ideal for gardens in which a relaxed, informal ambience is desired. Rosemary and Bay Laurel create permanency, while Angelica introduces seasonal height and dominance towards the back of the border. Where space allows, both herbaceous and annual herbs can be planted or sown.

Are herbs suitable for cottage gardens?

PLANNING A COTTAGE HERB GARDEN

Mixing vegetables and herbs with flowers and fruit trees is sometimes known as *potage gardening*, as well as *edible landscaping* in North America. Attractive displays of these and other plants in a cottage-garden setting need not just be in a bed between a path and a hedge or fence (see below), but with gravel or other informal paths meandering through a larger area.

Runner beans, perhaps scrambling up netting, rustic arches or pyramids of informal poles, can be used to create backgrounds, as well as sectioning off areas. Towards the middle and end of summer, Sweetcorn, with its tassel-like seedheads, also forms a screen and is an ideal background for herbs with feathery foliage, such as Dill and Fennel.

Informal stepping-stone paths within the cottage-garden area are inexpensive options that enable herbs to be reached.

Clusters of evergreen herbs create dominant features, especially when they are in flower.

WHICH PLANTS TO USE

Informality and irregularity are the keys to planning a cottage herb garden. If the proposed area has a few apple or pear trees in it, herbs and other decorative plants can be planted around them. If, however, the area is clear of plants, there is a further option of just having an irregular medley of herbs. Use the plant spacings indicated in the A–Z of culinary herbs (see pages 26–65) to help with your planning.

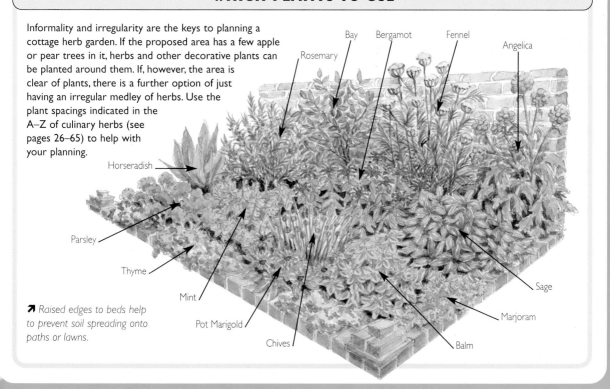

Bay   Bergamot   Fennel   Angelica

Rosemary

Horseradish

Parsley

Thyme

Mint

Pot Marigold

Chives

Balm

Marjoram

Sage

↗ *Raised edges to beds help to prevent soil spreading onto paths or lawns.*

Herbs in containers

Will all herbs grow in containers?

Many herbs can be grown in containers, including Rosemary, an evergreen shrub with aromatic leaves and mauve flowers, and Bay, which is often grown as a half-standard in tubs. Some herbs are not suitable for containers and these include the tall and dominant Angelica, a biennial with large, umbrella-like flowerheads. However, many lower-growing types are ideal, from Chives to Parsley, while Mints, with their invasive roots, are especially suitable.

USING CONTAINERS FOR HERBS IN YOUR GARDEN

Medleys of herbs within a single container, together with other herbs growing in individual pots, can create most attractive features. Differently sized, shaped and coloured pots provide variety for the eye.

These are ideal for small, terraced and courtyard gardens, as well as for balconies and roof gardens.

- Tubs, pots, troughs and growing-bags are ideal on patios and positioned near to kitchen doors.
- For balconies, where the container has to be both decorative and functional, planters with cupped holes in their sides are ideal. Troughs and pots are other possibilities, but ensure that water can escape without dripping onto balconies below.
- Windowboxes planted with low and bushy herbs create colour and flavours throughout summer.
- Tubs and large pots are ideal for half-standard Bay trees; when positioned either side of an entrance they create a memorable feature. Rosemary in a rustic half-tub is also attractive throughout summer. For a quick display, put three or five small plants in a tub.

Position culinary herbs in pots close to kitchen doors for convenience.

ADVANTAGES AND DISADVANTAGES OF HERBS IN CONTAINERS

Advantages

✔ Ideal for small gardens and balconies.

✔ Roots of spreading or invasive herbs, such as Mints, can be constrained.

✔ Containers such as planters with cupped holes can be planted with different herbs – ideal for small gardens. Windowboxes also make good homes for several different herbs.

✔ Tender herbs can be moved under cover in early winter.

Disadvantages

✘ Containers need regular attention and watering.

✘ Compost in containers may become overheated in summer.

✘ Some containers may need to be replanted every year.

Herbs for containers

Some herbs are especially suited to certain containers – here is a guide to choices that will give assured results. Variegated forms of Mint, as well as colour-leaved Sages and Thymes, introduce extra colour.

Growing-bags
Mints (pages 46–48); Sage (page 59), when young.

Hanging-baskets
Parsley (page 54); Thyme (page 64).

Pots and planters
Basil (page 51); Chives (page 28); Mints (pages 46–48); Parsley (page 54); Sage (page 59), when young; Thyme (page 64).

Troughs and windowboxes
Chives (page 28); Marjoram (page 52); Mints (pages 46–48); French Tarragon (page 35).

Tubs
Bay (page 43); Rosemary (page 56); Sage (page 59).

GETTING PLANTS STARTED IN CONTAINERS

To ensure success with herbs, it is essential to plant them in suitable containers (suggestions for plants are given opposite). If the container was used during the previous season, it must be thoroughly washed. Also check the drainage holes to make sure they are not blocked.

Composts

Where compost has to give stability to containers, such as tubs and pots that are homes to large, leafy plants, use loam-based compost with extra sharp sand. Lighter-weight composts, such as peat-based types, are ideal for windowboxes.

Pots

Rosemary
Parsley
Sage
Green Basil
Purple Basil

↰ *Mints are ideal for pots – divide and replant when congested.*

↗ *Many culinary herbs can be grown in pots, especially when the plants are young.*

↗ *Chives are ornamental as well as being widely used in cookery.*

Troughs

Tarragon   Marjoram   Variegated Applemint
Purple-leaved Sage

↗ When positioned at ground level and planted with tall herbs, troughs often need the stability created by loam-based compost. When they are secured to railings or placed on balconies, however, lighter peat-based compost is the better option.

BAY TREES

A strong wooden tub or large pot and loam-based compost are essential for success with a Bay tree. Before planting and filling the tub or pot, place it in the desired position, since it will be too heavy to move later.

◀ Make sure stems are well secured

Windowboxes

Chives   Bay   Pot Marjoram
Sage
Parsley

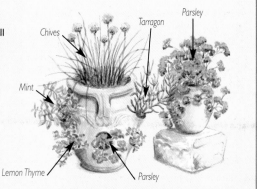

↗ Windowboxes are ideal for low, spreading and trailing herbs. If used outside a casement window (where the frame opens outwards), check that it will not damage the plants.

Growing-bags

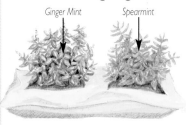

Ginger Mint   Spearmint

↗ These are bought complete with their own compost; cut 'windows' in the top, add water and plant the herbs. Where growing-bags are reused, top up with peat and add a light dusting of fertilizer.

Ornate planters

These containers – with cupped holes in their sides – are ideal for small gardens and balconies, because they enable a mixture of herbs to be grown in the same container. Loam-based compost, with extra sharp sand and ample drainage in the base of the container, assures long-term success.

Chives   Tarragon   Parsley
Mint
Lemon Thyme   Parsley

Ornamental planters with cupped holes in their sides can be homes to a wide range of herbs.

Growing herbs indoors

Several herbs are ideal for life on a windowsill indoors, and these include those indicated below. Some herbs, such as **Pot Marjoram** and **Basil**, can be lifted from a herb garden in autumn, put in pots and encouraged to grow indoors during winter. Roots of **Mint** lifted in autumn, potted up and placed in gentle warmth in a greenhouse, will provide fresh leaves in winter. In addition, these useful plants introduce unexpected colour to kitchens, especially in winter.

Are herbs easily grown indoors?

Small culinary herbs in separate pots are ideal for windowsills indoors.

SINGLE-PLANT POTS

When growing herbs on windowsills, do not put several different types in the same pot or planter, because herbs that have been harvested will need to be removed and replaced by others. Small pots are also easier than large ones to accommodate on narrow and short windowsills.

Containers

Both clay and plastic pots suit herbs. However, plants in plastic pots usually need less water than those in clay types, where moisture evaporates through the sides and helps to keep the compost cool. Therefore, water each plant individually. Decorative outer pots make plants more attractive.

Positions

Avoid windowsills exposed to strong and direct sunlight; dappled sunlight is better. Do not use steamy positions and those exposed to cold draughts.

RANGE OF SUITABLE HERBS

Culinary herbs are mainly hardy garden plants. Most of them, when mature, are too large for growing in pots on a windowsill, but a few are worth considering. Pots of herbs are often available from garden centres, as well as food supermarkets, and provide leaves over a long period.

Allium schoenoprasum **(Chives)**
Mid-green, tubular, grass-like leaves (see page 28). Clump-forming plant that is easily grown.

Anthriscus cerefolium **(Chervil)**
Bright green, fern-like leaves (see page 32) that resemble those of Parsley. It is essential to have young plants.

Ocimum basilicum **(Basil)**
Bright green, aromatic leaves with grey-green undersides (see page 51). Pleasant clove-like flavour.

Origanum onites **(Pot Marjoram)**
Bright green, aromatic leaves and a sprawling nature (see page 53); raised as a hardy or half-hardy annual.

Petroselinum crispum **(Parsley)**
Bright green, deeply divided, curly, tightly packed leaves (see page 54). If flowers appear, cut them off.

Satureja hortensis **(Summer Savory)**
Dark green, spicy-flavoured leaves borne on square, hairy stems (see page 60), and lilac-coloured flowers.

Thymus vulgaris **(Thyme)**
Dwarf, spreading, evergreen herb with leaves that have a slightly spicy and sweet flavour (see page 64).

Colour-themed herb gardens

If you have to buy plants, a colour-themed bed will be costly. However, plants can be easily and inexpensively raised from cuttings (see below). Young, colourful and variegated, large-leaved **Sages** are superb, as well as slightly feathery herbs to create shape and colour contrasts. Variegated **Thymes** are also useful. Do not expect a colour-themed herb garden to have a wide range of herbs, as plants are invariably selected solely for their attractive leaves.

Is a colour-themed bed practical?

RAISING SAGE PLANTS

To create a instant display with Sages, it is essential to have enough young, bushy plants that can be spaced 13–15 cm (5–6 in) apart. In early autumn, take 7.5 cm (3 in) long cuttings with 'heels'. Insert them in pots of equal parts moist peat and sharp sand; place in a cold frame. In spring, nip out the growing points to encourage bushy growth. These can be planted in mid- or late spring.

Sages with colourful leaves

Salvia officinalis
Sage
Grey-green

Salvia officinalis
'Purpurescens'
Purple-leaved Sage
Suffused purple

Salvia officinalis
'Icterina'
Variegated Sage
Green and gold

Salvia officinalis
'Tricolor'
Variegated Sage
Grey-green, splashed creamy-white

COLOUR-THEME DESIGNS

A patchwork pattern

➜ Sages are short-lived shrubs that become straggly and have to be replaced every 3–4 years. However, when in a colour-theme design they will probably need replacing earlier. The initial stage of this design is to create a diagonal, railway (railroad)-like framework of *Buxus sempervirens* 'Suffruticosa' (Dwarf Box), an evergreen shrub; space plants 15–23 cm (6–9 in) apart. Sages can then be planted in spring in colourful patterns. Regular trimming is essential to prevent plants intruding on their neighbours.

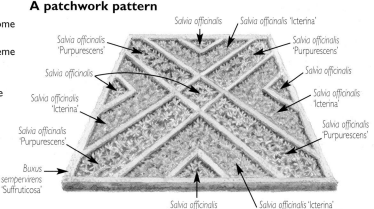

Salvia officinalis
'Purpurescens'

Salvia officinalis

Salvia officinalis 'Icterina'

Salvia officinalis
'Purpurescens'

Salvia officinalis

Salvia officinalis
'Icterina'

Salvia officinalis
'Purpurescens'

Salvia officinalis
'Icterina'

Buxus sempervirens 'Suffruticosa'

Salvia officinalis

Salvia officinalis 'Icterina'

Contrasting segments

➜ Circular designs planted with colour-contrasting herbs are ideal for a bed cut out of a lawn, or one that is surrounded by crazy paving (cleft stones) or gravel. Use *Salvia officinalis* 'Purpurescens' (Purple-leaved Sage) to line the edges, spokes and inner circle, with other colours in between.

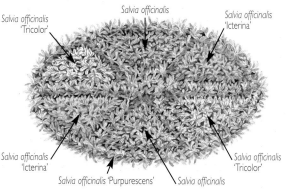

Salvia officinalis
'Tricolor'

Salvia officinalis

Salvia officinalis
'Icterina'

Salvia officinalis
'Icterina'

Salvia officinalis 'Purpurescens'

Salvia officinalis

Salvia officinalis
'Tricolor'

Relaxed designs

Informal arrangements of herbs, perhaps in circular designs, are easier to create and involve less maintenance than regimented designs. They can have height contrasts and, perhaps, involve the blue-green and feathery foliage of Fennel above a sea of colour-contrasting herbs.

Nosegay gardens

What is a nosegay?

Anosegay is a bunch or posy of fragrant flowers, ranging in type from scented herbs to redolent garden flowers. The term *nosegay* derives from the early English word *nose*, meaning fragrance, and *gay*, implying toy or ornament. However, the term has now come to mean a bouquet or posy of redolent flowers and encompasses many aromatic herbs. Some herbs give off fragrance through their flowers, and others through their leaves.

COMFORTING FRAGRANCES

In the same way that some colours, such as light blue, have a relaxing and comforting effect, so too have many fragrances. Sweet, honey-like, lavender and fruit-like redolences of nosegay gardens have a gentle and soothing nature, making their presence known, but not intrusively.

CAN HERBS AND OTHER NOSEGAY PLANTS BE GROWN TOGETHER?

As long as a nosegay plant does not trespass on its neighbour's area and overwhelm it with leaves, these plants can be grouped together. Choose a wind-sheltered position and one that is not at risk from late-season frosts. Well-drained, moisture-retentive soil is an advantage, but with moderate fertility.

Try a medley of permanent plants, such as Rosemary and Lavender (both will create a fragrant, flowering, internal garden hedge), with ephemeral ones like scented annuals, which create opportunities to change plants from one year to another. Within this design, culinary herbs with scented flowers and aromatic leaves can be used. Herbs with coloured leaves, such as Sages and Thymes, can be added to create further eye appeal. To unify the whole area, surround it with a low hedge formed of the popular *Buxus sempervirens* 'Suffruticosa' (Dwarf Box).

POSY OR NOSEGAY?

A posy is a small bunch of flowers, usually fragrant, and a more recent term for a nosegay.

A NOSEGAY HERB GARDEN

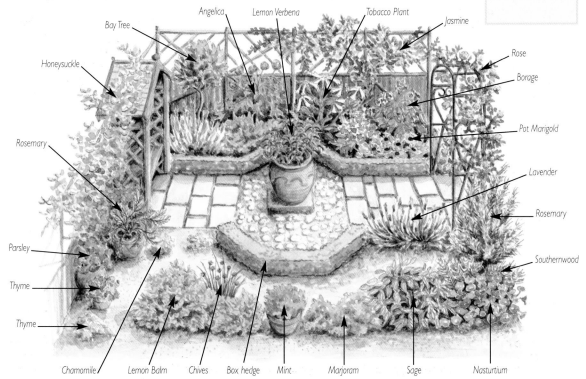

Richly fragrant gardens are oases of rest and relaxation; in a large garden, screen off a wind-sheltered area and use a medley of scented plants, plus herbs.

CONTAINERS IN NOSEGAY GARDENS

Containers can be added to nosegay gardens, as well as being used to create cloistered and scented features on patios. A tub or large container and planted with *Rosmarinus officinalis* (Rosemary) makes an eye-catching feature with a cottage-garden feel (see left). This evergreen shrub is described on page 56. When Rosemary is cut and the stems are taken indoors the room is filled with a rich, slightly camphor-like aroma. Incidentally, when cutting it for room decoration, hammer the stem ends flat and place overnight in water in a cool room.

Chamaemelum nobile (Chamomile; also known as *Anthemis nobilis*), which yields an essential oil and is used for flavouring liqueurs and making Chamomile tea, can also be grown in containers (see right). It has a light, feathery habit and is ideal for growing in ornate pots – a terracotta shade is preferable to a strong colour or white. Daisy-like, white flowers are produced on short stems during the summer months. For a banana-like redolence, use the form 'Treneague', which is non-flowering.

↗ *Rosemary creates a striking display in a large pot; or put three or five small plants in a tub.*

↗ *Put three* Chamaemelum nobile *(Chamomile) plants in a distinctive container; regularly pinch back stems to keep plants bushy.*

HOW TO MAKE A NOSEGAY OR POSY

Fragrant garden flowers and herbs can be used in many distinctive and colourful ways indoors. Apart from posies and table decorations (see right), they are ideal for brightening bedrooms and guest rooms. Scented posies also make excellent hand-held features for bridesmaids. The fragrant posy theme for a bridesmaid can also extend to a head-dress; cut a length of wire to encircle the head, cover the wire with florist's tape and secure colour-themed fragrant florets to it.

A nosegay (posy)

Sweet Scabious

Pot Marigold

Sweet Mignonette

A table-centre posy

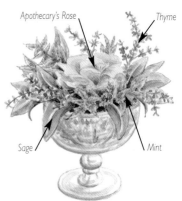

Apothecary's Rose

Thyme

Sage

Mint

↗ *A nosegay – or posy – is perfect for brightening a room, as well as making a lovely gift for a friend or relative.*

↗ *A fragrant posy adds a unforgettable quality to table displays and can be a focus of attention – and discussion!*

SCENTED ANNUALS

Nosegays and posies have a delicate and simple nature that encourages the use of non-dominant scented annuals. If large and exotic, colour-dominant flowers were chosen, they would overwhelm many annuals and destroy the innocent, everyday nature of posies.

Calendula officinalis (Pot Marigold; page 37) has a pungent aroma, while *Scabiosa atropurpurea* (Sweet Scabious) produces a warm, sweet, honeyed scent. The cottage-garden hardy annual *Reseda odorata* (Sweet Mignonette) was made fashionable in France by the Empress Josephine in the early nineteenth century. It later become popular in London windowboxes, and whole streets were said to be drenched in its ambrosial scent. Several stories surround this annual; it was highly esteemed by romantics, with a legend suggesting that good fortune attends a lover who rolls three times in a bed of Mignonette!

Herbs in flower arrangements

Fresh herbs are ideal for creating unusual flower and foliage arrangements. They are versatile, and combine sweet and refreshing fragrances with a wide range of shapes, colours and textures. Umbrella-like flowerheads formed of many small, individual flowers are just as captivating as those that are large and brightly coloured. Dried flowers are also candidates for long-term attractiveness and several of them are suggested on the opposite page.

Are herbs suitable?

HERBS FOR FLOWER ARRANGEMENTS

Many leafy and flowering herbs are ideal for arranging in pots and other decorative containers. Here are a few of them.

← *Borago officinalis* (**Borage**): somewhat oval leaves with silvery hairs. In addition to the leaves, it has attractive flowers (see page 36).

← *Calendula officinalis* (**Pot Marigold**): light green, spoon-shaped leaves and large, daisy-like, bright orange or yellow flowers (see page 37).

← *Melissa officinalis* (**Balm**): lemon-scented, nettle-shaped, light green leaves (see page 45). *Melissa officinalis* 'Aurea' (Golden-leaved Balm) has gold-and-green leaves.

← *Mentha* (**Mints**): several culinary Mints are ideal for flower arrangements (see pages 46–48). Most have an upright form and are useful for creating a distinctive outline.

← *Monarda didyma* (**Bergamot; also known as Bee Balm and Oswego Tea**): the mid-green, hairy, aromatic leaves introduce a superb foil (see page 49).

← *Rosmarinus officinalis* (**Rosemary**): evergreen shrub with narrow, dark green, aromatic leaves as well as distinctive flowers (see page 56).

← *Salvia officinalis* (**Sage**): aromatic, grey-green leaves and violet-blue flowers in early summer. There are purple and variegated forms (see page 59).

← *Thymus vulgaris* (**Thyme**): with trailing stems and handsome leaves, this herb is ideal for softening the edges of containers and unifying plants (see page 64).

UMBRELLA-LIKE FLOWERHEADS

When in flower arrangements, these distinctive flowerheads always capture the attention, especially as they invariably stand above the normal height of leaves and other flowers. Several popular herbs have this flower shape, including:

← *Anethum graveolens* (**Dill**): yellow flowers and blue-green leaves (see page 30).

← *Angelica archangelica* (**Angelica**): dominant flowerheads, best in large arrangements (see page 31).

← *Anthriscus cerefolium* (**Chervil**): white flowers and bright green leaves (see page 32).

← *Carum carvi* (**Caraway**): small, green flowers and fern-like leaves (see page 38).

← *Foeniculum vulgare* (**Fennel**): golden-yellow flowers and blue-green leaves (see page 40).

← *Pimpinella anisum* (**Aniseed**): white flowers and green leaves (see page 55).

HERB AND FLOWER ARRANGEMENTS

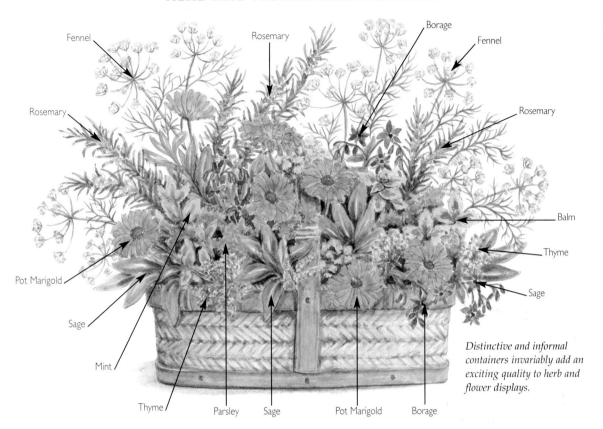

Fennel

Rosemary

Borage

Fennel

Rosemary

Rosemary

Balm

Thyme

Pot Marigold

Sage

Sage

Mint

Thyme

Parsley

Sage

Pot Marigold

Borage

Distinctive and informal containers invariably add an exciting quality to herb and flower displays.

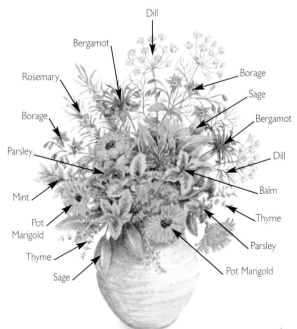

Dill

Bergamot

Borage

Rosemary

Sage

Borage

Bergamot

Parsley

Dill

Mint

Balm

Pot Marigold

Thyme

Thyme

Parsley

Sage

Pot Marigold

A medley of herbs, garden flowers and leaves seldom fails to capture and retain attention.

Dried herbs for flower arrangements

As well as introducing colour and interesting shapes to winter flower arrangements, dried herbs are ideal for adding a rural quality to well-ventilated kitchens. Where possible, hang bunches of herbs from ceilings; alternatively, suspend a basket of herbs.

Drying flowers Many herb flowers are easily dried, retaining most of their colour and scent. Usually, those formed of clusters of small flowers give the best result. Those with heavy flowerheads are best dried by standing them upright in a dry container in a warm, dry place. Others, such as Sage, Marjoram and Lavender, are best dried by tying them in bunches and suspending them in a warm, airy room.

Drying evergreen leaves The easiest way to dry evergreen leaves is to suspend them in bunches, again in a dry, airy room. Avoid placing them in a high temperature, where drying would be rapid. These herbs are best picked in summer, when they are in good condition.

Drying non-evergreen herbs These are dried in the same way as evergreen types, but the leaves rapidly lose moisture and shrivel and usually become too unattractive in arrangements. However, they are ideal for suspending from hooks and beams in kitchens, as well as adding to pot-pourri mixtures.

Herbs in pot-pourri

Pot-pourri is a mixture of fragrant dried petals, to which has been added a medley of aromatic herbs, spices and seeds. Essential oils are usually added. At one time, pot-pourri was used to cloak unpleasant medical odours, but today it is widely used to introduce fragrance to rooms. Ready-made pot-pourri mixtures are available from specialist shops, but if you have a herb garden it is exciting to use some of them as part of the ingredients.

How did pot-pourri originate?

Mixtures of flowers and leaves can be encouraged to create delightful, long-lasting fragrances.

The name pot-pourri is French and literally means 'rotten pot'. It refers to the original 'moist' method of creating pot-pourri, when layers of fresh flowers were fermented with salt to create a strongly scented and long-lasting mixture that would introduce fragrance to rooms. The mixture often had a muddy-brown appearance and containers were kept closed, except at intervals when lids were removed and the fragrances released. Today, dry pot-pourri is more popular. Incidentally, pot-pourri is pronounced *po-poo-ree*, and the plural of pot-pourri is pot-pourris.

After gathering leaves and flowers for use in pot-pourri, do not allow them to become dry before they are used.

Lidded containers are essential for 'moist' pot-pourri, retaining fragrant aromas until desired.

POTS FOR POT-POURRI

Attractive and interestingly shaped containers are an essential part of pot-pourri. These include porcelain, china, glazed earthenware and glass. Copper and brass containers are also attractive. Wooden containers can be used, but they absorb essential oils and fragrance from the mixture. Therefore, fit a china or porcelain dish inside the wooden container.

BOOSTING FRAGRANCE

The fragrance in dry pot-pourri diminishes after a few weeks, especially in a warm room and when the ingredients are fully exposed to the air. Rather than creating further dry pot-pourri, it is possible to rejuvenate the mixture by adding a few drops of essential oil.

Rapid fragrance

To scent a room rapidly, place the pot-pourri in a wide-based bowl, rather than a narrow and tall one. This exposes more pot-pourri to the air.

For rapid scenting, use a wide container.

ECONOMICAL POT-POURRI

Choose an ornamental, wide-based container and spread crumpled newspaper over the base. Add a level-surfaced piece of newspaper, on which a thin layer of pot-pourri can be arranged. Ensure that the newspaper cannot be seen through the pot-pourri.

CREATING DRIED POT-POURRI

Richly scented flowers form the main part of the pot-pourri. These usually are colourful, richly fragrant roses. Other fragrant flowers are added to the mix, including Lavender, Jasmine, *Philadelphus* (Orange-blossom), Honeysuckle and Carnations. To ensure the mixture is colourful and visually attractive, use shapely and colourful flowers such as Marigolds, Forsythia, Cornflowers, Forget-me-nots, Borage and Larkspur. Those from the many 'everlasting' flowers can also be added.

There are many recipes for dry pot-pourri and they can all be modified to ensure that the ingredients are readily available. One basic recipe is given below.

Ingredients

- 2 cups of dry rose petals
- 2 cups of dry Lavender flowers
- 1 cup of Cornflower petals
- 1 cup of Lemon Verbena leaves
- ½ cup of powdered orris root
- 1 tablespoon ground allspice
- 1 tablespoon ground cinnamon
- 1 tablespoon ground cloves
- few drops of essential rose oil

Method of preparing dried pot-pourri

➔ *Spread the ingredients out in a decorative bowl, taking good care not to crush them as you do so.*

- Mix all of the ingredients together, taking care not to squash and damage any soft-textured ones.
- Add a few drops of essential oil until the fragrance is strong enough. Then use a small pencil-like stick to mix the oil with the other ingredients.
- Place the entire mixture in a lidded jar. Shake the contents every other day, and in about six weeks it will have matured and be ready for transferring to decorative containers and placing in rooms. Add a few flowerheads to make it attractive and colourful.

➔ *Evenly spread a few drops of an essential oil over the ingredients; then carefully mix, using a thin stick or pencil.*

READY-MADE POT-POURRI

Apart from making your own pot-pourri, it is possible to buy a ready-made mixture. Here are a few tips about successful buying.

- Select a mixture with colours that complement the main room in which it will be placed.
- Check that the mixture still has a strong fragrance – and is one that you like.
- Only buy a mixture if it looks bright and fresh, and has not been in its container for too long.
- After buying, cover the container with plastic film to get it home without the mixture losing much of its fragrance to hot temperatures and drying wind.

ADDING CITRUS PEEL

Dried peel from grapefruits, limes, oranges and lemons are further fragrances for pot-pourri. The peel is easily prepared, but remember that it takes ten or more days to dry (depending on the temperature) and therefore needs to be prepared before the pot-pourri is created. Here is the way to prepare the peel.

- Remove the rind from a few fruits, scrape off the pith and cut into large pieces. A sharp knife or a potato peeler that is not blunt can be used for this task.
- Cover a tray with kitchen paper (towels), space out the pieces of peel and place in an airing cupboard (closet) to dry. When dry, store them in a jar with a screw-top lid.

Culinary herbs

What is the range of culinary herbs?

Everyone knows the popular herbs, such as Mint, Parsley, Sage and Thyme, but there are many others that introduce distinctive flavours to food, from meat and fish to stews and even bread. In this part of this book, 39 culinary herbs are described and illustrated, and their uses are explained. Many of them are best used fresh, but some can be dried or even frozen, and these techniques are described on pages 74–75. You can buy herbs from garden centres or specialist nurseries, or raise plants from cuttings and seeds or by division (see pages 66–71).

Finding the right herb

Plant entries in this A–Z section are arranged alphabetically according to their botanical names. The information on the right will help you find herbs that are mainly known by their common names. Some herbs have several common names, and these are featured in the main entry for each herb.

Allium sativum

GARLIC UK/USA

Height: 30–75 cm (1–2½ ft)
Spread: 23–30 cm (9–12 in)

Hardy, bulbous perennial, a member of the onion family and well known for its characteristic aroma and flavour. It has narrow, grey-green leaves and a bulbous base formed of several parts known as cloves. During early summer, plants produce globular heads of small, white, red-tinged flowers.

Culinary uses

Cloves of garlic are used to flavour many foods, including salads, fish and meat dishes, especially in continental Europe where it has an almost cult following. However, it needs to be used with care, as many people are allergic to it. Indeed, some French cooks claim that the use of Garlic cloaks the natural flavour of food and therefore should be used sparingly – if at all!

Bulbs formed of several cloves

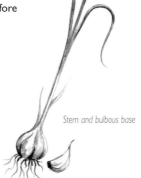

Stem and bulbous base

Raising new plants

Choose an area of light, fertile, well-drained but moisture-retentive soil, preferably manured during early winter and in full sun. The soil should have had time to settle before planting. In late winter, buy mature, healthy bulbs, ready for planting in early spring.

Plant individual cloves 15 cm (6 in) apart in drills 7.5 cm (3 in) deep and 23–30 cm (9–12 in) apart. Position each clove with its pointed end upwards, and its top just below the soil's surface. Do not just push the cloves into the soil, as this inhibits root development. Sometimes, whole bulbs are used, and these need wider spacings, as well as drills about 10 cm (4 in) deep.

Looking after plants

Keep the soil moist but not saturated, and free from weeds. Usually, plants are trouble-free.

Harvesting

In late summer, as the leaves and stems become yellow, carefully use a garden fork to lever bulbs from the soil. Leave them on the soil's surface to dry and ripen in the sun. Then, store them in string bags in a dry, frost-proof, cool shed.

Bulbs can also be tied into bundles and hung up.

Allium schoenoprasum

CHIVES UK/USA

Cive USA **Ezo-negi** USA **Schnittlauch** USA

Height: 15–25 cm (6–10 in)
Spread: 25–30 cm (10–12 in)
Hardy, perennial, clump-forming bulbous plant with grass-like, tubular, mid-green leaves and rose-pink flowers borne in dense, rounded heads at the tops of long stems during early and mid-summer.

Raising new plants

Chives form clumps which, after 3–4 years, are best carefully dug up and divided during early or mid-autumn. Replant young pieces from around the outside of the clump (discard the old inner part) and position about 30 cm (12 in) apart in light or moderately heavy, well-drained soil. They grow in full sun or light shade.

Alternatively, during spring and early summer, sow seeds thinly and evenly in drills that are 12 mm (½ in) deep and 30 cm (12 in) apart. Germination takes 2–3 weeks. When seedlings are large enough to handle, thin them to 15 cm (6 in) apart; later, transfer them to their growing positions, spacing them 30 cm (12 in) apart.

Culinary uses

The mild flavour of the leaves makes them ideal for flavouring soups, omelettes, egg and cheese dishes, as well as adding to sandwiches. When finely chopped, the leaves can be used as a garnish for mashed (creamed) potatoes; adding them to young, boiled potatoes produces a distinctive flavour. The leaves are also used as *fines herbes* and in *sauce tartare*.

Looking after plants

Keep the plants well watered throughout summer and remove flower stems to encourage the development of leaves. Plants die down to soil level in autumn and produce fresh leaves in spring.

Chives can also be grown in pots and windowboxes. When in pots they can be taken indoors in autumn and placed on a cool windowsill, where they provide leaves through to mid-winter.

Harvesting

Cut off leaves close to their bases; young leaves are always best. As well as being used fresh, leaves can be dried or frozen (see pages 74–75).

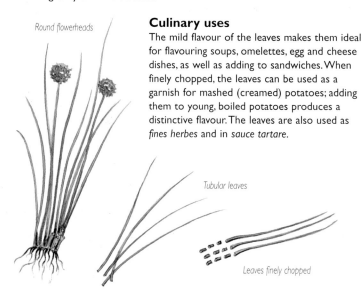

Round flowerheads

Tubular leaves

Leaves finely chopped

Aloysia triphylla

LEMON VERBENA UK/USA

Lemon-scented Verbena UK/USA

Height: 1.2–1.8 m (4–6 ft)
Spread: 90 cm–1.2 m (3–4 ft)
Also known as *Lippia citriodora*, this slightly tender, deciduous shrub generally needs the comfort of a cool greenhouse during winter. However, in warm, temperate areas it can be grown outdoors. It has pale to mid-green, aromatic, lance-shaped leaves and small, pale-mauve flowers during late summer. The leaves when bruised have a rich, lemon-like scent.

Culinary uses

The leaves have a wide range of uses, from stuffings to flavouring chicken and fish. It can be added to jellies and jams and makes a refreshing tea.

Pale mauve, tubular flowers

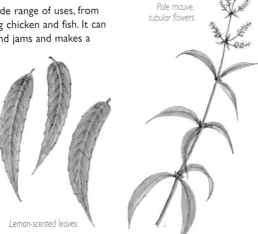

Lemon-scented leaves

Raising new plants

During mid-summer, take 7.5 cm (3 in) long cuttings from young sideshoots. Remove the lower leaves and trim their bases beneath the lowest leaf. Insert them in equal parts moist peat and sharp sand in pots, and place the pots in a warm propagating frame.

When rooted, transfer the young plants to pots and overwinter them in a frost-proof greenhouse or cold frame. Plant into a garden during the following late spring.

Looking after plants

Where plants are grown in large pots, repot them in spring every year. A sunny, wind-sheltered position is essential, as well as light, well-drained soil.

When plants are grown in the soil and in a cold area, cut them down in autumn and cover the roots with straw until spring. Alternatively, if in a pot move into a frost-proof greenhouse.

Where plants are growing strongly and in a warm area, and produce a permanent framework of branches, prune plants to within 30 cm (12 in) of the ground in spring; this will encourage the development of young shoots and leaves.

Harvesting

Pick the leaves throughout summer and use fresh. Alternatively, harvest leaves in late summer and store in airtight containers.

Anethum graveolens

DILL UK/USA

Height: 60–90 cm (2–3 ft)
Spread: 30–38 cm (12–15 in)
Also known as *Peucedanum graveolens*, this hardy annual has an upright habit, with hollow, ridged stems and blue-green, feathery, thread-like leaves that have an aniseed flavour. From early to mid-summer, it bears small, yellow, star-like flowers in umbrella-like heads up to 7.5 cm (3 in) wide.

Raising new plants

Choose well-drained, moderately fertile soil in a sunny position. From early spring to mid-summer, sow seeds evenly and thinly in 12 mm (½ in) deep drills about 30 cm (12 in) apart. Germination takes 10–14 days.

When the seedlings are large enough to handle, thin them to 7.5–10 cm (3–4 in) apart. Later, give the plants more space by thinning them to about 20 cm (8 in) apart.

Looking after plants

Keep the soil moderately moist, but not continually saturated, in order to encourage rapid growth. Also remove weeds; if left, they will take moisture and food from the soil surrounding the seedlings.

Culinary uses

Freshly picked leaves are usually used fresh to garnish and flavour fish, boiled potatoes, peas, beans, soups and poultry. They are also added to salads. The seeds have a distinctive aniseed flavour and are added to the vinegar when pickling gherkins.

Umbrella-like flowerheads

Thread-like leaves

Aniseed-flavoured seeds

Harvesting

Pick and use the leaves when young and fresh. The leaves are difficult to dry, but can be frozen (see page 75).

IMPORTANT NOTE

Do not grow Dill and Fennel close together, because it is difficult to identify self-sown seedlings.

Angelica archangelica

ANGELICA UK/USA

Archangel USA   Garden Angelica USA   Wild Parsnip USA

Height: 2.1 m (7 ft)
Spread: 90 cm–1 m (3–3½ ft)
Hardy biennial or short-lived perennial, invariably grown as the former. It forms a dominant feature in a herb garden as well as in a mixed border. Large, light shiny-green, deeply indented leaves are borne on thick, ridged, tough stems. In mid- and late summer, the plant develops yellow-green, umbrella-like flowerheads about 7.5 cm (3 in) across.

Culinary uses
The stems are candied and used in cake decoration.

Raising new plants

In spring, sow seeds thinly and evenly in outdoor seedbeds, in drills 6 mm (¼ in) deep and 25–30 cm (10–12 in) apart. When seedlings are large enough to handle, transplant them to 30 cm (12 in) apart in rows similarly spaced.

In early spring of the following year, transfer the plants to their final growing positions.

Looking after plants

After planting in rich soil in a sunny or partially shaded position, keep the soil moist and free from weeds. To encourage the development of strong stems, remove the flower-heads. Plants that are not allowed to produce flowers will live into the following year.

Harvesting

In early summer, cut the main stems while still tender and before the plants flower; sideshoots can also be cut in late summer. Cut off the leaves and stems.

Large, dominant flowerheads

Large, shiny, green leaves

Stems can be candied

Anthriscus cerefolium

CHERVIL UK/USA

Salad Chervil USA

Raising new plants

Chervil is a biennial, but is usually grown as a hardy annual in order to encourage the production of young leaves. From late spring to mid-summer, sow seeds thinly and evenly in shallow drills that are 30 cm (12 in) apart and where plants are to grow. Germination takes 2–3 weeks. When the seedlings are large enough to handle, thin them first to 15 cm (6 in) apart, and later to 30 cm (12 in).

To ensure a regular supply of young leaves, sow seeds every 4–5 weeks. Always use fresh seeds, as these have a better chance of germination than those that are over a year old.

Height: 30–45 cm (12–18 in)
Spread: 30–38 cm (12–15 in)
Hardy biennial with bright green, fern-like leaves with a slight resemblance to those of Parsley. The ridged stems are strongly aromatic and hollow. In its second year, and from early to late summer, it displays umbrella-like heads, up to 7.5 cm (3 in) wide, of white flowers.

Looking after plants

Keep the soil moderately moist, especially during dry periods; this helps to prevent the development of seeds. Also pinch out the flower buds if seeds are not wanted.

Culinary uses

The leaves, with their delicate aniseed flavour, are used to garnish salads and sandwiches, as well as to flavour salads, soups, egg and fish dishes. Dried leaves are also used in stuffings, as well as in *fines herbes* for omelettes. Leaves can be used fresh, dried or frozen.

White flowers

Ridged stems

Bright green leaves

Dried leaves used in stuffings

Harvesting

Cut off the leaves when young; these have the best flavour. The leaves can also be dried, and this is best when the leaves are cut about eight weeks after seeds were sown.

Armoracia rusticana

HORSERADISH UK/USA

Great Railfort UK Mountain Radish UK/USA Red Cole UK/USA

Raising new plants

Once planted, Horseradish can be left in position for several years. However, it becomes invasive and therefore is often planted fresh each year (taking care to remove all roots when they are harvested in early autumn).

Deeply cultivated, fertile, well-drained soil in full sun or light shade is essential. In early spring, use a dibber (dibble) to make holes about 30 cm (12 in) deep; space them 60–75 cm (24–30 in) apart, if growing several plants. Insert a piece of root (known as a thong) into each hole, and firm the soil. The top of each thong should be about 5 cm (2 in) below the soil's surface. These thongs are about finger-thick and 23–30 cm (9–12 in) long.

If plants are left in the soil for several years, there is no need to plant fresh pieces annually.

Height: 45–60 cm (18–24 in)
Spread: 45–75 cm (18–30 in) – roots often spread wider

Also known as *Cochlearia armoracia*, this hardy, long-lasting herbaceous perennial has wide-spreading roots and therefore is best given a bed on its own. Small, white, cross-shaped flowers appear in early summer among large, rough-surfaced, wavy-edged or lobed, dark green leaves, about 45 cm (18 in) long. However, it is grown for its long, yellowish-buff roots that have a pungent, peppery flavour.

Culinary uses

The roots, when crushed, are grated or minced and simmered with milk, vinegar and seasoning to make a peppery sauce to flavour meat, fish and salads. It is widely used with beef.

Pungently flavoured roots

Long roots

Harvesting

Roots can be lifted as required throughout summer. However, in mid-autumn, when the leaves are starting to die, lift the remaining roots, wash them and allow them to dry. Then store them in dry sand or peat in a box in a dry, cool, dark place such as a shed.

In mild areas, the roots can be left in the soil throughout the winter and harvested when required. However, lift them by mid-spring, because if left they will become hollow and inedible.

Artemisia abrotanum

SOUTHERNWOOD UK/USA

Lad's Love UK **Old Man** UK/USA **Southern Wormwood** USA

Height: 60 cm–1.2 m (2–4 ft)
Spread: 60 cm–1.2 m (2–4 ft)
Hardy shrub with an erect habit, and deciduous or semi-evergreen depending on the climate. It develops attractive downy, grey-green and finely divided leaves, which emit a strong, apple-like fragrance when crushed. During mid- and late summer it bears round, dull yellow flowers in slender clusters; in cool climates, however, the flowers seldom appear.

Culinary uses
Although not now widely employed as a herb, it was traditionally used as an ingredient in herbal teas.

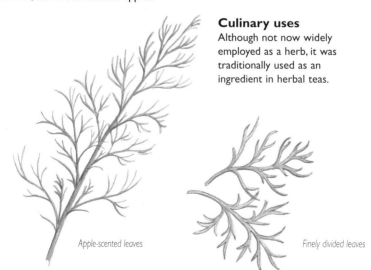

Apple-scented leaves   *Finely divided leaves*

Raising new plants
During late summer, take 7.5–10 cm (3–4 in) long, semi-hardwood cuttings, preferably with a heel (a small piece of the older wood) attached to the base. Insert these in pots of equal parts moist peat and sharp sand, and place in a cold frame for the duration of winter.

In spring, pot up the rooted cuttings into individual pots and place outdoors until late summer or early autumn, when they can be planted into a herb garden.

Looking after plants
Keep the soil moist and free from weeds. In mid-spring of each year, cut all stems to within 15–20 cm (6–8 in) of the soil. This initiates the development of young shoots and leaves. The young shoots and leaves are frost-tender, however, so do not prune back the plant until all risk of frost has passed.

Harvesting
Throughout the summer months, pick leaves as required. They can be used fresh or dried.

Artemisia dracunculus

FRENCH TARRAGON UK

Estragon USA **Tarragon** UK/USA

HORIZON HERBS © RICHO CECH

Height: 45–60 cm (18–24 in), sometimes more
Spread: 30–38 cm (12–15 in), sometimes more
Hardy perennial, with a bushy nature and aromatic, grey-green leaves with a sweet, mint-like taste and aroma. In late summer, it develops lax clusters of small, greenish-white, rounded flowers; in temperate climates they do not fully open.

Culinary uses

This herb is best known as a flavouring in Tarragon vinegar, but the leaves are also used fresh in salads and are a basic part of *fines herbes*. It is used in the preparation of French mustard and *sauce tartare*. Further uses include flavouring chicken and other white meats, and adding to sauces for fish dishes.

Sweet and mint-like taste and aroma

Greenish-white flowers

Stems create a bushy plant

Raising new plants

Every three years, renew the plants. In early or mid-spring, lift and divide established plants, replanting young pieces (rhizomes) from around the outside of the clump and putting them 5–7.5 cm (2–3 in) deep and 30–38 cm (12–15 in) apart.

Plants can also be raised from seeds, but these are said not to have such aromatic leaves as plants raised by division. An alternative is to take 5–7.5 cm (2–3 in) long cuttings from the base of the plant in spring and insert them in pots of equal parts moist peat and sharp sand. Place in gentle warmth; when rooted, reduce the temperature and place in a cold frame until they can be planted into a herb garden.

Looking after plants

Plants can be left in place for about three years, but the flavour of the leaves is best on young plants. Pinch off the flower stems as soon as they appear.

The essential oil in French Tarragon disappears when the herb is dried. For this reason, the plants are sometimes lifted in autumn, put in large pots and placed in a greenhouse; this provides fresh leaves for use during winter.

Harvesting

Use leaves fresh, picking them from early to late summer. Leaves can be cut and dried, but in the process they lose some of their aroma. They can also be frozen (see page 75).

Borago officinalis

BORAGE UK/USA

Cool-tankard UK/USA Talewort UK/USA

HORIZON HERBS © RICHO CECH

Height: 45–90 cm (1½–3 ft)
Spread: 30–38 cm (12–15 in)
Hardy annual with oval, green leaves smothered in rough, silvery hairs. From early to late summer, it bears clustered heads of blue flowers; there are also pink and white-flowered forms. The flowers are often used in herbal flower arrangements.

Culinary uses
Borage leaves and flowers are often added to cold drinks, including claret cup. Two or three leaves placed in a jug impart a refreshing flavour, resembling that of cucumber. It can also be added to salads.

Raising new plants
From mid-spring to mid-summer, sow seeds evenly and thinly in shallow drills where the plants are to grow. Space the drills 30 cm (12 in) apart.

When the seedlings are large enough to handle, thin them to 25–38 cm (10–15 in) apart.

Sowing seeds every 4–6 weeks ensures a regular supply of young leaves right through the summer.

Looking after plants
Keep the soil moist throughout summer. Plants often produce self-sown seedlings; these are best removed to stop plants becoming congested. Remove all weeds.

Harvesting
Pick leaves when young and use them fresh. It is possible to dry them, but this is difficult and they often become black.

Used to flavour salads and cold drinks

Flowers added to cold drinks

Hairy leaves and stems

Calendula officinalis

POT MARIGOLD UK/USA

English Marigold UK/USA   Marigold UK/USA

Raising new plants

From mid- to late spring, sow seeds where they are to germinate and grow; sow thinly and evenly in drills 12 mm (½ in) deep and 25–30 cm (10–12 in) apart. When seedlings are large enough to handle, thin them to 30 cm (12 in) apart.

This plant will often produce masses of self-sown seedlings too.

Looking after plants

Although it survives in poor soils, it produces best growth and flowers when in well-drained but moisture-retentive soil in full sun. Remove dead flowerheads to encourage others to develop.

Height: 45–60 cm (18–24 in)
Spread: 30–38 cm (12–15 in)
Popular hardy annual with a bushy but erect habit and light green, narrowly spoon-shaped leaves. From late spring or early summer to the first frosts of autumn, it displays large, daisy-like, bright orange or yellow flowers up to 10 cm (4 in) wide. The leaves and stems have a pungent aroma. For garden ornamentation there are many cultivars, in a mixture of pastel shades. As well as being grown in garden borders, it is often raised in pots and this, of course, is reflected in its common name.

Harvesting

Throughout the summer months, pick flowers and remove the petals either for immediate use or for drying (see pages 74–75). Only use fresh, young leaves in salads.

Erect and bushy stems

Culinary uses

The petals have been used to colour butter and soft cheeses, as well as to add colouring to rice and soups. The chopped leaves are used as a salad ingredient, and the flowers as a salad garnish.

Confusing Marigolds

Do not confuse *Calendula officinalis*, the popular Pot Marigold, with French and African Marigolds, which are *Tagetes* species.

Daisy-like flowers, with double as well as single forms

Light green, spoon-shaped leaves

Carum carvi

CARAWAY UK/USA

Height: 60–75 cm (24–30 in)
Spread: 38–45 cm (15–18 in)

Dried seeds used to add flavour to food

Feathery, mid-green leaves

Hardy biennial with aromatic, feathery, fern-like, mid-green leaves which have an aniseed-like flavour. During early and mid-summer, small green flowers appear in umbrella-like heads. These are followed by seeds. Seeds are sown one year to produce plants that will develop flowers and seeds during the following year.

Culinary uses

Dried seeds are used to flavour cakes, bread and buns (rolls), as well as cheese dishes and salads. They are added to lamb and pork when roasted. Sausages and cabbages also benefit from them. Seeds are also used to flavour Kümmel, a colourless German liqueur, while oil of Caraway is distilled from the fruits and often used as a flavouring agent.

Upright stems bearing green flowers

Raising new plants

During late summer, sow seeds evenly and thinly in shallow drills, 30–38 cm (12–15 in) apart, where plants are to grow and flower.

When the seedlings are large enough to handle, thin them to 30 cm (12 in) apart.

Looking after plants

During the second year, Caraway grows vigorously and develops mid-green, fern-like leaves. In mid-summer, small, green flowers appear in umbrella-like heads, followed by seeds. A sunny position is essential to encourage their development and ripening.

Harvesting

As soon as the seeds ripen, cut down the entire plant to ground level. Tie the stems into small bundles and hang upside-down in a dry, cool, airy place until the seedheads are dry – indicated by them falling off. At this stage, it is essential to put paper bags over them or a large piece of paper underneath them.

Gather the seeds and pass them through a sieve to remove the fine, dust-like material.

Coriandrum sativum

CORIANDER UK/USA

Chinese Parsley USA Cilantro USA Parsley USA

Height: 23–75 cm (9–30 in)
Spread: 15–20 cm (6–8 in)
Hardy annual with an erect but branching habit, dark green, somewhat feathery, fern-like leaves and pink-mauve flowers during mid-summer. These develop seeds which are used as flavourings.

Culinary uses
The spicy-flavoured leaves are used in food such as soups, broths and meat dishes, while the seeds add a distinctive taste to curries and stews. The seeds are also used in liqueurs, in perfumery, in the manufacture of soap, and in curry powder. Unripe green seeds, as well as the leaves, have a strange, unpleasant odour, but this is replaced by a sweet, aromatic bouquet on ripening. Seeds are reddish-brown when ripe.

Umbrella-like flowerheads

Seeds added to liqueurs

Dark green leaves

Raising new plants
New plants are raised each year. In mid- and late spring, sow seeds evenly and thinly in shallow drills, 30 cm (12 in) apart. Germination takes 2–3 weeks; when seedlings are large enough to handle, thin them to 15 cm (6 in) apart.

Looking after plants
Coriander (Cilantro) will grow on most soils, but avoid those that are excessively fertile and have recently been manured, as this encourages over-lush growth. A sunny, open position is essential to promote rapid ripening.

Plants flower in mid-summer and the seeds ripen during late summer. Keep the soil moist, but not continually saturated.

Harvesting
When grown commercially, seeds are harvested when about two-thirds of the seedheads have turned from green to grey. However, home gardeners can harvest the seeds slightly later. Stems are cut and the seedheads dried under cover. Rub out the seeds and store them either whole, or ground into a powder.

Foeniculum vulgare

FENNEL UK/USA

Height: 1.5–2.1 m (5–7 ft)
Spread: 45–75 cm (18–30 in)
Hardy herbaceous perennial with a dominant appearance and thread-like, bright green to blue-green leaves and golden-yellow flowers packed in umbrella-like heads, 10 cm (4 in) across, during mid- and late summer.

Culinary uses
The leaves are used to flavour fish dishes, as well as in salads and with vegetables, while the strongly aniseed-flavoured seeds are added to cakes, bread and soups.

Flowers   *Seeds*

Aniseed-flavoured seeds

Filigreed, thread-like leaves

Upright stems with umbrella-like flowerheads

IMPORTANT NOTE
Do not grow Fennel and Dill close together, as it is difficult to identify self-sown seedlings.

Raising new plants
Select a well-drained, moderately fertile position and in mid- or late spring sow seeds evenly and thinly in shallow drills spaced 38–45 cm (15–18 in) apart. Incidentally, when plants are primarily grown for their seeds, sow seeds in early spring; this enables seeds to be gathered in autumn. Germination is not rapid. When the seedlings are large enough to handle, thin them to 30–38 cm (12–15 in) apart.

Another way to increase this herb is to lift and divide congested plants in spring, as soon as shoots appear. Replant young pieces from around the outside of the clump, setting them 38–45 cm (15–18 in) apart.

Looking after plants
Unless seeds are needed, pinch off all flower stems to prevent their development. Keep the soil fairly moist and free from weeds.

Harvesting
Pick the leaves fresh in summer. They are quite difficult to dry satisfactorily, but can be gathered while fresh and then frozen (see page 75).

Where plants are grown for their seeds, do not remove the flower-heads; gather the seedheads in late autumn, just before they are fully ripe. They need to be dried slowly; therefore, spread the seedheads on white paper and allow them to dry naturally. Turn them daily. When the seeds have separated, place them in dry, airtight jars in a cool cupboard.

Glycyrrhiza glabra

LIQUORICE UK/USA

Licorice USA Sweetwood UK/USA

HORIZON HERBS © RICHO CECH

Height: 60–90 cm (2–3 ft)
Spread: 60–90 cm (2–3 ft), or more
Hardy, deeply rooted, herbaceous perennial, belonging to the pea family and with leaves formed of 9–17, mid- to deep green, oval leaflets. The bean-shaped flowers are pale blue or bluish-purple, borne in clusters and followed by small pods, up to 2.5 cm (1 in) long and containing 3–4 seeds. The roots are invasive, often spreading several metres and, on light soil, reaching a depth up to 90 cm (3 ft).

Culinary uses
Liquorice is grown for its dried rhizomes (specialized underground roots) and normal roots. They have been used as a flavouring agent to cloak less pleasant ingredients, and in powdered form or as a liquid extract for making sweets (candies), soft drinks, cough mixtures and pastilles.

Versatile roots
As well as providing a distinctive flavour, in North America the roots have been used in the manufacture of boards for making boxes.

Raising new plants
During early and mid-spring, plant young suckers, spacing them about 30 cm (12 in) apart.

Looking after plants
Light, fertile, well-drained soil encourages rapid growth, as well as making harvesting easier. Keep the soil free from perennial weeds. There is little growth, about 23 cm (9 in), during the first year after being planted, but in the second season plants produce dense foliage that helps to suppress weeds.

In each autumn, as soon as the leaves fall off plants, cut the stems down to ground level.

Harvesting
When grown commercially, plants are left in place for 3–5 years. Harvesting of roots and rhizomes takes place in autumn.

Spreading and invasive roots

Strongly flavoured roots (rhizomes)

Hyssopus officinalis

HYSSOP UK/USA

HORIZON HERBS © RICHO CECH

Height: 45–60 cm (18–24 in)
Spread: 30–38 cm (12–15 in)
Hardy, partially evergreen perennial with an upright, branching and bushy habit. It is grown for its young, aromatic, mid-green leaves that have a mint-like flavour. From mid- to late summer, plants bear purple-blue, tubular flowers. There are also white and pink forms.

Culinary uses
The young leaves, which can be picked throughout the year, are used fresh in a wide range of foods, or dried and mixed in stuffings. The leaves are at their best just before the flowers open. Fresh leaves are put in salads, as well as fresh or dried in soups and stuffings. In cooked dishes, they are used to 'balance' oily fish or fatty meats.

Branching, bushy stems

Aromatic, mint-flavoured leaves

Raising new plants
In mid- and late spring, sow seeds evenly and thinly in a seedbed. Sow in drills 6 mm (¼ in) deep and 30 cm (12 in) apart. Germination takes 2–3 weeks. When seedlings are large enough to handle, thin them to 15 cm (6 in) apart. In early autumn, lift plants and put them into their growing positions, about 30 cm (12 in) apart.

The other way to increase Hyssop is to take 6.5–7.5 cm (2½–3 in) long cuttings in late spring and insert them in pots of equal parts moist peat and sharp sand. Place in a cold frame, and when rooted pot up into individual pots. Plant in a herb garden in late summer or early autumn.

Looking after plants
Light, well-drained soil in full sun or light shade is essential. Keep the soil moist and free from weeds and, every 3–4 years, replace plants with young ones.

Harvesting
Pick the leaves throughout the year and, preferably, use them when fresh. Leaves can also be dried, but pick them when young.

Laurus nobilis

BAY UK/USA

Bay Laurel UK/USA **Grecian Laurel** USA **Laurel** USA **Sweet Bay** UK/USA

Height: 1.8–3.6 m (6–12 ft)
Spread: 1.8–3.6 m (6–12 ft)

Hardy, evergreen shrub or tree with aromatic, glossy, mid- to dark green leaves. As a tree it is dominant and can exceed the height and spread suggested above. However, it is often grown as a half- or full standard, either in soil in a herb garden or in a large tub. It is often used as a centrepiece in a cartwheel garden.

Evergreen leaves

Culinary uses

The aromatic leaves are added to a wide range of food, including fish, rice dishes and stews. They are also a basic part of *bouquet garni*. Leaves can be dried, but this needs to be done slowly to prevent their colour fading.

Used to flavour many foods

Raising new plants

During late summer and early autumn, take 10 cm (4 in) long heel cuttings from lateral shoots. Trim their bases below a leaf-joint, remove lower leaves, insert in pots of equal parts moist peat and sharp sand and place in a cold frame.

When rooted, transfer them to individual pots of loam-based compost. Overwinter them in a cold frame and plant in a growing position or a large pot about two years later.

Looking after plants

Well-drained but moisture-retentive soil and a position in full sun suit Bay. It needs protection from cold winds which, during severe winters, may damage the leaves and shoots.

When grown as a half- or full standard in a tub or border, plants need to be shaped a couple of times during summer. They also need to be supported by strong stakes.

Harvesting

Pick and use leaves as required. When young and newly picked, leaves are slightly bitter, but become sweet as they dry.

When drying them, put in a dark place to ensure their rich colours are retained.

Levisticum officinale

LOVAGE UK/USA

Italian Lovage UK   Old English Lovage UK

Height: 90 cm–1.2 m (3–4 ft)
Spread: 60–75 cm (24–30 in)
Earlier known as *Ligusticum levisticum*, this tall, hardy perennial has large, divided, mid-green, Parsley-like leaves and clusters of yellowish pale-green flowers borne in large, umbrella-like heads. The leaves have a strong flavour, resembling that of yeast and celery.

Culinary uses
The stems are sometimes blanched and used in a similar way to celery, while young stems are candied in the same way as for Angelica. The leaves can be chopped and used to flavour soups, stews and stocks, while raw young leaves are often added to salads. The seeds are aromatic and used in vegetable dishes and baking.

Raising new plants
The easiest way to increase Lovage is to lift and divide congested plants in autumn or spring; replant young pieces from around the outside of the clump.

Alternatively, during mid- and late spring sow seeds in shallow drills in a seedbed. When seedlings are large enough to handle, thin them to 30 cm (12 in) apart; in autumn, transfer plants to their growing positions, 90 cm (3 ft) apart.

Looking after plants
Fertile, moisture-retentive but well-drained soil in a sunny position suits this herb best. Keep the soil free from weeds.

Harvesting
Pick young leaves in spring and early summer for immediate use, as well as for drying and freezing.

Tall stems bearing yellowish, pale green flowers

Aromatic seeds

Stems are candied

Deeply divided, mid-green leaves

Melissa officinalis

BALM UK/USA

Bee Balm USA Common Balm UK/USA Lemon Balm USA Sweet Balm USA

Height: 60–75 cm (24–30 in)
Spread: 30–45 cm (12–18 in)
Hardy herbaceous perennial, grown in herbaceous borders as well as in a herb garden for its lemon-scented, nettle-like, wrinkled, tooth-edged, pale-green leaves. During early and mid-summer it bears tiny, white, tubular flowers.

Melissa officinalis 'Aurea' (Golden Balm), which has decorative gold-and-green leaves, is used to add flavour to cold drinks.

Culinary uses
From spring to autumn use young, fresh leaves to flavour cold drinks and fruit salads. Leaves can also be dried (see pages 74–75).

Attractive nettle-like leaves

White, tubular flowers

Lemon-scented leaves

Raising new plants
Lift and divide congested plants in autumn or early spring. Replant young pieces from around the outside of the clump; discard old and woody central parts.

Looking after plants
Plants are usually healthy, but slugs and snails can wreak havoc in shaded areas. Plants die down to ground level in autumn and send up fresh shoots in spring. In autumn or winter, remove old stems.

To encourage the Golden Balm to produce attractive leaves from mid-summer onwards, cut all stems to 15 cm (6 in) above the ground in the latter part of early summer.

Harvesting
Pick young, fresh leaves throughout summer, as needed. Leaves can also be dried, but need to be picked before the plant flowers.

IMPORTANT NOTE
Melissa officinalis *should not be confused with* Monarda didyma *(Bee Balm), which is often grown in herbaceous and mixed borders, and is featured on page 49.*

Mentha spicata

SPEARMINT UK/USA

Common Mint UK

HORIZON HERBS © RICHO CECH

Height: 45–60 cm (18–24 in)
Spread: Spreading and invasive
Also known as *Mentha viridis*, this hardy, herbaceous perennial has leaves with a distinctive spearmint flavour. The leaves are mid-green and prominently veined. From mid-summer to early autumn, plants bear pale-purple flowers in dense whorls up the stems.

Culinary uses
The leaves have a mint-like aroma and flavour, and are frequently used in mint sauce. Leaves are also used to make a refreshing tea. Sprigs are often added to cold drinks and to flavour vegetables, especially potatoes and peas.

Flowers borne in whorls

Branching stems

Prominently veined leaves

Raising new plants
Lift and divide congested clumps in early or mid-spring and replant young pieces taken from around the outside. Space them about 20 cm (8 in) apart.

Alternatively, during late spring take 7.5–10 cm (3–4 in) long cuttings from the base of the plant and insert them in pots of equal parts moist peat and sharp sand. Place them in a cold frame or cool greenhouse until rooted, then plant in a herb garden or container.

Looking after plants
Fertile, moisture-retentive soil in a warm, sheltered, shaded position suits Spearmint. Each winter the shoots die down; remove these in late winter or early spring.

Because this plant spreads rapidly, it is advisable to grow it either in 15–20 cm (6–8 in) wide, bottomless pots, plunged to the rim in border soil, or in containers.

Harvesting
Pick and use leaves while young and fresh. Alternatively, they can be dried (see pages 74–75).

Mentha suaveolens

APPLEMINT UK/USA

Apple-scented Mint UK **Round-leaf Mint** UK/USA

Height: 45–60 cm (18–24 in)
Spread: Spreading and invasive
Also known as *Mentha rotundifolia*, this hardy herbaceous perennial has round, almost egg-shaped leaves with an apple-like aroma and flavour. The pale green leaves are smothered in white hairs. From mid-summer to early autumn it bears pale purple flowers in dense whorls up the stems.

Culinary uses

The leaves, with their apple-like aroma and flavour, are used in mint sauce. Indeed, it is often said that it is superior to *Mentha spicata* (Spearmint) in the making of mint sauce. Leaves are also used to make a refreshing tea, while sprigs are added to cold drinks and to flavour vegetables.

Flowers borne in dense whorls

Leaves have an apple-like aroma

Raising new plants

Lift and divide congested clumps in early or mid-spring and replant young pieces taken from around the outside. Space them about 20 cm (8 in) apart.

Alternatively, during late spring take 7.5–10 cm (3–4 in) long cuttings from the base of the plant and insert them in pots of equal parts moist peat and sharp sand. Place in a cold frame or cool greenhouse until rooted, then plant in a herb garden or container.

Looking after plants

Fertile, moisture-retentive soil in a warm, sheltered and shaded position suits this herb. Each winter the shoots die down, and these need to be removed in late winter or early spring.

Because this plant spreads rapidly, it is advisable to grow it either in 15–20 cm (6–8 in) wide, bottomless pots, plunged to the rim in border soil, or in containers.

Harvesting

Pick and use leaves while young and fresh. Alternatively, they can be dried (see pages 74–75).

Mentha suaveolens 'Variegata'

PINEAPPLE MINT UK/USA

Height: 30–45 cm (12–18 in)
Spread: Spreading and invasive
Also known as *Mentha rotundifolia* 'Variegata', this hardy, herbaceous perennial is closely related to Applemint but with leaves that have creamy-white edges and a pineapple aroma. It is slower-growing and has a slightly sprawling habit.

Culinary uses
The leaves have a slight pineapple aroma and taste, and are added to drinks.

Further Mints to consider
Apart from Spearmint, Applemint and Pineapple Mint, others have exciting and unusual flavours.

Mentha x gracilis: earlier known as *Mentha x gentilis*, and popularly as Ginger Mint, with reddish-purple stems and bright green and yellow variegated leaves that impart a ginger-like redolence when bruised.

Mentha requienii: known as Peppermint, it forms a carpet of small, pale green leaves that when bruised emit a peppermint aroma. Occasionally, it is known as Spanish or Corsican Mint.

Raising new plants
Lift and divide congested clumps in early or mid-spring and replant young pieces taken from around the outside. Space them about 20 cm (8 in) apart.

Alternatively, during mid- and late spring take 5–7.5 cm (2–3 in) long cuttings from the base of the plant and insert them in pots of equal parts moist peat and sharp sand. Place them in a cold frame or cool greenhouse until rooted, then plant in a herb garden or container.

Looking after plants
Fertile, moisture-retentive soil in a warm, sheltered and shaded position suits this plant. Each winter the shoots die down, and these need to be removed in late winter or early spring.

Because this plant spreads rapidly, it is advisable to grow it either in 15–20 cm (6–8 in) wide, bottomless pots, plunged to the rim in border soil, or in containers.

Harvesting
Pick and use leaves while young and fresh. Alternatively, they can be dried (see pages 74–75).

Creamy-white edges to the leaves

Pineapple-flavoured leaves

Monarda didyma

BERGAMOT UK/USA

Bee Balm UK/USA **Oswego Tea** UK/USA **Sweet Bergamot** UK/USA

Height: 60–90 cm (2–3 ft)
Spread: 38–45 cm (15–18 in)
Hardy herbaceous perennial with mid-green, oval to lance-shaped, hairy, aromatic leaves. From early summer to early autumn it bears dense whorls of bright scarlet flowers.

Culinary uses
Add young, freshly gathered leaves to summer drinks, salads or pot-pourri. Leaves are also used in pork dishes, and the flowers can be added to salads.

Raising new plants
The easiest way to increase this border plant is by lifting and dividing congested plants in autumn or spring and replanting young pieces from around the outside. Discard the old, inner parts.

Another way to increase it is by sowing seeds in gentle warmth in a greenhouse in early or mid-spring. When the seedlings are large enough to handle, transfer them to wider spacings in seed-trays (flats) and later plant them in a nursery bed, 23 cm (9 in) apart. In autumn, transfer plants to their growing positions in beds and borders.

Looking after plants
Fertile, moisture-retentive soil in full sun or light shade suits Bergamot best. Keep the soil free from weeds and mulch the soil to keep it cool and moist, and to suppress weeds.

Harvesting
Pick the leaves when young and just before plants flower. Use them fresh or dried (see pages 74–75).

Aromatic leaves

Ideal for planting in a flower border, as well as in a herb garden

Flowers are added to salads

Myrrhis odorata

SWEET CICELY UK/USA

Anise UK/USA **Cow Chervil** UK **Garden Myrrh** UK/USA **Great Chervil** UK

Myrrh UK/USA **Sweet Chervil** UK/USA **Sweet Fern** UK

HORIZON HERBS © RICHO CECH

Raising new plants

Plants readily produce self-sown seedlings. Alternatively, during mid- and late spring sow seeds shallowly in drills where the plants are to grow.

When they are large enough to handle, thin the seedlings to about 60 cm (2 ft) apart.

Looking after plants

Grow in fertile, moisture-retentive soil in full sun or partial shade. Keep the soil moderately moist and free from weeds.

Height: 60 cm–1 m (2–3½ ft)
Spread: 60–75 cm (2–2½ ft)
Hardy, herbaceous, erect perennial with light to mid-green, fern-like, aromatic leaves that have a sweet, aniseed-like aroma and flavour. The early and mid-summer, umbrella-like heads, up to 5 cm (2 in) wide, of small, white flowers later yield seeds that are used to flavour foods.

Culinary uses

The aniseed-flavoured leaves are used in fruit dishes and added to salads. They are claimed to reduce the acidity of fruit. The seeds are used to flavour fruit dishes, while the thick tap root is eaten raw or cooked as a vegetable.

Harvesting

Pick young leaves during spring and early summer for using fresh. Alternatively, they can be dried (see pages 74–75).

Gather seeds in summer, and dry or pickle them.

Leave digging up the roots for use as a vegetable until late summer or autumn.

Aromatic, fern-like leaves

Seeds used to flavour fruit dishes

Tap root sometimes eaten as a vegetable

Ocimum basilicum

BASIL UK/USA

Common Basil UK/USA Sweet Basil UK/USA

THOMPSON & MORGAN

Height: 30–45 cm (12–18 in), sometimes more
Spread: 30–38 cm (12–15 in)

Attractive, bright green leaves
and branching stems

Clove-flavoured leaves

Half-hardy annual with four-sided stems and bright green, aromatic leaves that have grey-green undersides. White flowers appear in late summer. The strongly clove-flavoured leaves are used to introduce an unique piquancy to food.

Culinary uses

The leaves are used fresh or dry in omelettes, salads, fish dishes, soups and minced (ground) meat. It is also popular in Italian tomato dishes and in *pesto* – herb-based Italian flavourings used with pasta. Historically, Basil was an essential part of turtle soup, as well as the once famous Fetter Lane sausages in London.

Raising new plants

During early or mid-spring, sow seeds thinly and evenly in pots or seed-trays (flats) in a greenhouse with a temperature of 13°C (55°F). Use well-drained seed compost. When the seedlings are large enough to handle, transfer them to wider spacings in seed-trays (flats).

Slowly acclimatize plants to lower temperatures and transfer to a herb garden in late spring or early summer, setting them 30–38 cm (12–15 in) apart.

Basil dislikes being disturbed, however, and an alternative way to raise plants is to sow seeds directly in their growing places in late spring, in drills 6 mm (¼ in) deep. When the seedlings are big enough to handle, thin them in stages to 30–38 cm (12–15 in) apart.

Looking after plants

Grow in well-drained but moisture-retentive soil in a warm, sheltered position. Keep the soil moist, but not continually saturated.

Nip out the flowers to encourage the development of good foliage.

Harvesting

Pick leaves fresh, as desired. Leaves can also be dried and frozen (see pages 74–75).

Origanum majorana

MARJORAM UK/USA

Annual Marjoram USA Knotted Marjoram UK Sweet Marjoram UK/USA

Height: 45–60 cm (18–24 in), sometimes less
Spread: 30–45 cm (12–18 in), sometimes less
Slightly tender perennial with a bushy and shrubby habit; in temperate climates it is invariably grown as a hardy or half-hardy annual. The bright green leaves cluster around red, four-sided stems, with clusters of mauve, pink or white tubular flowers from early to late summer. The aromatic leaves appear from knot-like leaf joints.

Culinary uses

Young shoots and leaves are used to flavour meat or poultry, as well as in stuffings and omelettes and salads. They are used fresh or dried. Leaves have a stronger flavour when dried and are frequently used in pot-pourri. Marjoram is also a traditional part of *bouquet garni*.

Bright green leaves borne on slightly branching stems

Leaves are used fresh or dried to flavour foods

Raising new plants

When raised as a half-hardy annual, sow seeds evenly and thinly 3 mm (⅛ in) deep in pots or seed-trays (flats) during late winter or early spring. Keep the temperature at 50–59°F (10–15°C) and slowly reduce this after germination.

When the seedlings are large enough to handle, transfer them to wider spacings in a seed-tray (flat) and gradually harden them off. Later, plant in a herb garden.

Alternatively, sow seeds 6 mm (¼ in) deep in drills 23–30 cm (9–12 in) apart during late spring or early summer, where the plants are to grow. Later, thin the seedlings to 23–30 cm (9–12 in) apart.

Looking after plants

Well-drained, moisture-retentive soil and a warm, sheltered position are essential. Plants survive winter in mild areas, but it is usually best to pull them up in autumn and raise fresh plants the following year.

Harvesting

Pick leaves and stems as required; this is best done before the flowers open. They can be used fresh, or dried or frozen (see pages 74–75).

Origanum onites

POT MARJORAM UK/USA

Height: 30 cm (12 in)
Spread: 30 cm (12 in)
Hardy, perennial, low, often sprawling, bushy sub-shrub with bright green, aromatic leaves. Invariably, it is grown as a hardy or half-hardy annual. It is easily differentiated from *Origanum majorana* by its more branching habit and the reddish tinge suffusing the entire plant. It also has lilac flowers, which first appear slightly later than those of *Origanum majorana*.

Raising new plants

When raised as a half-hardy annual, sow seeds evenly and thinly 3 mm (⅛ in) deep in pots or seed-trays (flats) during late winter or early spring. Keep the temperature at 50–59°F (10–15°C) and slowly reduce this after germination.

When the seedlings are large enough to handle, transfer them into wider spacings in a seed-tray (flat) and harden them off. Later, plant in a herb garden.

Alternatively, sow seeds 6 mm (¼ in) deep in drills 23–30 cm (9–12 in) apart during late spring or early summer, where the plants are to grow. Later, thin the seedlings to 23–30 cm (9–12 in) apart.

Looking after plants

Fertile, moisture-retentive but well-drained soil is needed. Keep the soil evenly moist and free from weeds.

Leaves are used to flavour many foods

Culinary uses
The young leaves are used fresh or dried, in stuffings, as well as to flavour meat or poultry, soups, omelettes and sausagemeat. They are also popularly used with veal.

Branching stems bearing aromatic leaves and lilac flowers

Harvesting

Pick the leaves and stems as and when required; this is best done before the flowers open. They can be used fresh, or dried or frozen (see pages 74–75).

Petroselinum crispum

PARSLEY UK/USA

THOMPSON & MORGAN

Raising new plants

Parsley is usually raised by home gardeners as a hardy annual, sowing directly into the positions where plants will grow. From early spring to mid-summer, sow seeds thinly and evenly about 6 mm (¼ in) deep in a seed bed in a herb garden. Germination is slow, but this can be made more rapid by watering the seed drills with hot water before seeds are sown. Initially, thin the seedlings to 7.5 cm (3 in) apart, and later to 23 cm (9 in).

Sowing in pots is another way to raise new plants; sprinkle several seeds on loam-based compost and lightly cover them. Water carefully and place on a sunny windowsill.

Height: 30–60 cm (1–2 ft)
Spread: 23–38 cm (9–15 in)
Hardy biennial invariably grown as an annual. It is a well-known and widely grown culinary herb, with bright green, deeply divided, curly leaves that are tightly packed together. If left to grow naturally, without any trimming, it develops greenish-yellow flowers, but these are best removed as soon as they appear.

Looking after plants

A warm position in full sun or light shade suits it, and light, fertile, well-drained but moisture-retentive soil assures success. Keep the compost moderately moist and cut off flower stems. In late summer, cut down plants and water thoroughly to encourage fresh growth; cover them with cloches.

Culinary uses
The leaves are widely used in sauces and salad dressings, as well as being an essential ingredient of *bouquet garni*. They are also used to garnish sandwiches.

Greenish-yellow flowers

Distinctive, deeply divided, curly leaves

Leaves are used in sauces or as a garnish

Harvesting

Pick leaves when young; this also encourages the development of further leaves. Leaves can also be dried or frozen (see pages 74–75).

Pimpinella anisum

ANISEED UK/USA

Anise UK/USA **Common Anise** UK/USA

Raising new plants

During mid-spring, sow seeds in drills 6 mm (¼ in) deep and 38 cm (15 in) apart. Germination takes up to three weeks.

When the seedlings are big enough to handle, thin them to 30 cm (12 in) apart.

Looking after plants

A sheltered position in full sun and light, moderately fertile, well-drained but moisture-retentive soil is best.

Height: 38–45 cm (15–18 in)
Spread: 38–45 cm (15–18 in)
Hardy annual with a dainty appearance and brilliant green, feathery, finely divided, tooth-edged foliage. During mid- and late summer it develops umbrella-like flowerheads bearing small, white flowers. In cool temperate climates it is unlikely that the seeds will ripen; but growing it for seeds might become possible with global warming.

Culinary uses
The aromatic, small, hard, greyish-brown seeds have long been used to add flavour to cakes, sweets (candies), drinks and soups. Aniseed is a central part of the liqueur 'Anisette', as well as an ingredient in cough mixtures and lozenges.

Harvesting

This plant flowers in mid- and late summer, and following a warm summer the seeds ripen in autumn. Cut down the plant and thresh out the seeds. Then dry them in trays (flats) positioned outdoors in full sun or indoors in gentle warmth and with a flow of air.

When dry, they are greyish-brown, with a sweet and spicy taste and an agreeable aroma.

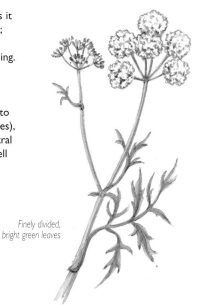

Strongly flavoured seeds

Finely divided, bright green leaves

Umbrella-like flowerheads

Rosmarinus officinalis

ROSEMARY UK/USA

THOMPSON & MORGAN

Height: 1.5–2.1 m (5–7 ft)
Spread: 1.2–1.5 m (4–5 ft)

An evergreen shrub, slightly tender in cold areas, with narrow, aromatic, mid- to dark green leaves. During mid- and late spring – and sporadically through to late summer and sometimes into early winter – it bears mauve flowers. It is ideal for growing in a border, as well as in a large herb garden. It can also be grown as an informal hedge.

Culinary uses

The leaves are used fresh or dried to introduce further flavour to pork, lamb and veal, as well as poultry, eggs and fish. Rosemary is also added to stuffings and sauces. However, remember that if used excessively it can overwhelm the natural flavour of food.

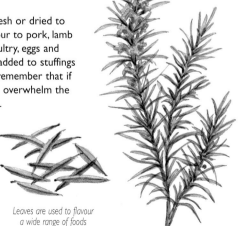

Mauve, lipped flowers borne in clusters along stems

Leaves are used to flavour a wide range of foods

Raising new plants

Initially, established plants can be bought from nurseries and garden centres. However, after 3–4 years plants often become bare around their bases and are best replaced. During mid-summer, take 7.5–10 cm (3–4 in) long cuttings and insert them in pots of equal parts moist peat and sharp sand. Place them in a cold frame.

When rooted, repot them into individual pots and replace in a cold frame, where they can be overwintered. In late spring, plant them into a border or herb garden.

Looking after plants

Little attention is needed, other than cutting out dead shoots in early spring and shortening straggly growths. If plants become over-grown, they can be cut back by about half in mid- or late spring.

Harvesting

The leaves are used either fresh or dried. When used fresh, remove them as needed.

To dry the leaves, cut whole stems and hang them in a dry, cool room. Unfortunately, dried leaves lose some of their flavour.

Rumex scutatus

SORREL UK/USA

French Sorrel UK/USA Garden Sorrel UK/USA

Height: 30–45 cm (12–18 in)
Spread: 20–25 cm (8–10 in)
Slender, semi-erect and slightly prostrate perennial with mid- to grey-green, somewhat triangular leaves that have an acid flavour. They often appear in dense clusters. The plant also develops clusters of small, green to red flowers.

Culinary uses
Young leaves, which have a lemon-like flavour, are added to sandwiches, salads and soup, while older leaves are cut and cooked liked spinach. They can also be made into a purée and served with fish and rich meats. In France, they are used in Sorrel soup, as well as to flavour sauces and omelettes.

Raising new plants
The easiest way to increase plants is to lift and divide congested clumps in spring or late summer; replant the young pieces about 20 cm (8 in) apart in rows 30 cm (12 in) apart.

Alternatively, sow seeds evenly and thinly in drills 6 mm (¼ in) deep and 30 mm (12 in) apart in a seed bed outdoors in mid-summer. When the seedlings are big enough to handle, thin them first to 7.5 cm (3 in) apart, and later to 23 cm (9 in).

Looking after plants
Keep plants free from weeds and nip off flowers to encourage the development of fresh leaves.

Harvesting
Cut off fresh, young leaves as and when they are needed.

They can also be dried and frozen in bags (see pages 74–75).

Distinctive, somewhat triangular leaves

Tiny, red to green leaves

Lemon-flavoured leaves

Ruta graveolens

RUE UK/USA

Common Rue USA Herb of Grace UK/USA

HORIZON HERBS © RICHO CECH

Height: 60–75 cm (24–30 in)
Spread: 45–60 cm (18–24 in)

Hardy, evergreen shrub with deeply divided, blue-green leaves that have an acrid flavour. During early and mid-summer – and sometimes into late summer – it bears clusters of sulphur-yellow flowers at the ends of young shoots. It is, however, the leaves, with their acrid and bitter nature, that are added to food.

Culinary uses

Young leaves are finely chopped and added to salads. However, take special care not to use this herb excessively.

*Leaves impart an acrid
and bitter flavour*

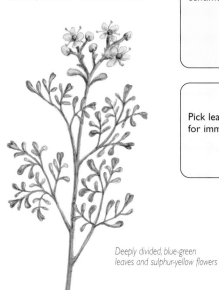

*Deeply divided, blue-green
leaves and sulphur-yellow flowers*

Raising new plants

Fresh plants can be raised from seeds and cuttings. Sow seeds in drills 3–6 mm (⅛–¼ in) deep in a seed bed outdoors during spring. When the seedlings are large enough to handle, thin them to 23–30 cm (9–12 in) apart. Later, transplant them to 45 cm (18 in) apart in either a herb garden or a mixed border.

Alternatively, take 7.5–10 cm (3–4 in) long cuttings from sideshoots during mid-summer. Insert them in pots of equal parts moist peat and sharp sand and place in a cool greenhouse. When rooted, transfer them to individual pots and overwinter in a cold frame.

Looking after plants

Plants need little attention, other than cutting off dead flowers in autumn. To keep plants low, use garden shears in spring to cut shoots back to within a few centimetres of the old wood.

Harvesting

Pick leaves when young and fresh, for immediate use or for drying.

Salvia officinalis

SAGE UK/USA

Common Sage UK/USA Garden Sage UK/USA

HORIZON HERBS © RICHO CECH

Height: 45–60 cm (1½–2 ft)
Spread: 45–60 cm (1½–2 ft)

Hardy, evergreen shrub with wrinkled, aromatic, grey-green leaves that impart a bitter taste. Small, tubular and very attractive violet-blue flowers appear during early and mid-summer, often totally covering the leaves. In addition to this species, there are several attractive forms with purple or variegated leaves. These are best grown in an ornamental part of a garden or to create colour in colour-leaved herb gardens (see page 19).

Culinary uses

The leaves have many uses in kitchens; they were traditionally used with fatty meats such as duck, goose and pork. Perhaps Sage is best known as part of stuffings, however, as well as being used with cheese, veal, liver and onions. It is extensively used in Italian cooking, as well as in other Mediterranean countries.

Violet-blue flowers

Branching stems

Aromatic leaves

Raising new plants

Sage is usually increased by cuttings in early autumn. Take cuttings from the current season's growth on healthy plants, forming cuttings 7.5 cm (3 in) long, with heels, and insert them in pots of equal parts moist peat and sharp sand. Place them in a cold frame.

When rooted, pot the cuttings up individually in loam-based compost and replace in a cold frame until spring. In late spring, plant them into a herb garden.

Looking after plants

Plants are usually short-lived and best replaced after 3–4 years. Trim plants back annually in late summer to prevent them becoming straggly, with bare centres.

Harvesting

Sage is harvested by pulling off leafy shoots and tying them in bunches. The leaves are either used fresh or hung up and encouraged to dry quickly in a warm room. Store leaves in airtight jars.

Satureja hortensis

SUMMER SAVORY UK/USA

Raising new plants

Raise new plants annually. During mid-spring, form drills 6 mm (¼ in) deep and about 23 cm (9 in) apart, and sow seeds evenly and thinly. Germination takes 2–3 weeks; when the seedlings are large enough to handle, thin them to 15–23 cm (6–9 in) apart.

Looking after plants

Well-drained, fertile soil and a position in full sun or partial shade suit this herb.

Discard plants in early winter.

Height: 30 cm (12 in)
Spread: 23 cm (9 in)
Hardy annual with a bushy habit and spicy-flavoured dark green leaves borne on square, hairy stems. From mid-summer to early autumn tiny, tubular, lilac-coloured flowers are produced from the leaf joints.

Culinary uses

The leaves are used to flavour meat and fish, as well as soups, egg and cheese dishes, drinks and stuffings. In France, Summer Savory is used when cooking broad (fava) beans.

Harvesting

Pick leaves throughout the summer and use fresh.

To dry leaves for winter use, cut down plants in late summer; tie them into bunches and hang up in a dry place.

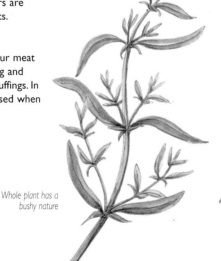

Whole plant has a bushy nature

Leaves are strongly flavoured and should be used sparingly

Satureja montana

WINTER SAVORY UK/USA

HORIZON HERBS © RICHO CECH

Raising new plants

During mid- to late spring, sow seeds evenly and thinly in drills 6 mm (¼ in) deep and 30 cm (12 in) apart. When the seedlings are large enough to handle, thin them to 23–30 cm (9–12 in) apart.

Looking after plants

Keep the soil free from weeds, and replace plants every 2–3 years.

Harvesting

Pick leaves throughout the summer and use fresh.

To dry leaves for winter use, cut down plants during late summer; tie them into bunches and hang up in a dry place.

Height: 30 cm (12 in)
Spread: 25–30 cm (10–12 in)
Hardy perennial, slightly resembling Rosemary, with an erect, bushy and woody nature and square-sectioned stems. The leaves are grey-green. From mid-summer to mid-autumn it bears rose-purple, tubular-shaped flowers from the upper leaf joints.

Culinary uses

The leaves are used in a similar way to Summer Savory, but the flavour is coarser. They are used to flavour meat and fish, as well as soups, egg and cheese dishes, drinks and stuffings.

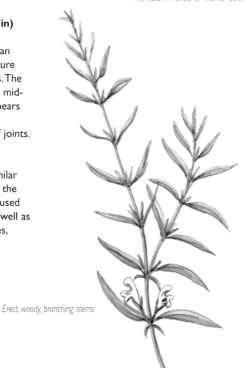

Erect, woody, branching stems

Leaves are used to flavour a wide range of foods

Tanacetum balsamita

ALECOST UK/USA

Balsam Herb UK **Costmary** UK/USA **Mace** UK **Mint Geranium** USA

HORIZON HERBS © RICHO CECH

Height: 60–90 cm (2–3 ft)
Spread: 45 cm (18 in)

Also known as *Chrysanthemum balsamita*, this hardy, herbaceous perennial produces somewhat oval to oblong, bluntly tooth-edged, matt-green leaves up to 15 cm (6 in) long, and tall flowering stems that bear rather loose clusters of mainly yellowish flowers. However, in cool areas it seldom produces flowers and rarely or never sets seed.

Culinary uses

The spicy, aromatic leaves have been used in salads, as well as in a herbal tea. Historically, it was used to flavour ales (see below).

Raising new plants

Lift and divide congested clumps in autumn or spring, and replant young pieces from around the outside.

Looking after plants

Keep the soil moist and free from perennial weeds.

Harvesting

Remove young leaves as and when they are required.

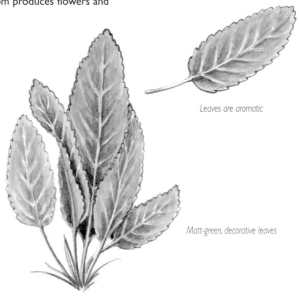

Leaves are aromatic

Matt-green, decorative leaves

Flavouring ale

In previous centuries, the leaves of this herb were added to ale to impart a spicy flavouring. In 1616, the magazine *The Countrie Farmer* said that both 'Costmarie and Avens' gave flavour to ales. This was at a time when 'ale' was synonymous with parish festivals, with brews such as Whitsun-ales, church-ales and lamb-ales (to celebrate the shearing of lambs) being popular. Indeed, the word 'bridal' is really 'bride-ale', meaning ale for the wedding feast.

Tanacetum vulgare

TANSY UK/USA

Common Tansy USA Garden Tansy USA Golden Buttons USA

Height: 90 cm–1 m (3–3½ ft)
Spread: 45–60 cm (18–24 in)
Hardy, erect perennial with deeply divided and serrated, dark green leaves, about 23 cm (9 in) long, and bright yellow, button-like flowers from mid- to late summer, which can be dried for use in winter flower arrangements. It has a very informal, cottage-garden appearance.

Culinary uses
The leaves can be shredded and used in omelettes, sandwiches and cheese dishes. They have also been used in traditional puddings and cakes, such as Easter Tansy Puddings, which were made with eggs and young Tansy leaves. Tansy tea was made by infusing the herbs in boiling water.

Strewing herb
Tansy was traditionally used as a strewing herb on floors of castles and large houses to create a fragrant atmosphere. It is also reputed to keep away flies, and an old moth powder recipe included Tansy, Rosemary and Thyme. A combination of Elder leaves and Tansy was also used.

Raising new plants
The easiest way to increase Tansy is to lift the often matted roots in late winter or early spring and divide them.

Alternatively, sow seeds in shallow drills, about 6 mm (¼ in) deep, in early spring. When the seedlings are large enough to handle, thin them to 30–45 cm (12–18 in) apart.

Looking after plants
It is a robust and persistent plant, but take care to remove weeds that might congest it. It has a creeping rootstock and is best confined to a secluded part of a garden, or grown in a bottomless bucket.

Harvesting
Pick leaves fresh throughout the summer months.

Stiff, upright stems

Deeply divided leaves

Thymus vulgaris

THYME UK/USA

Common Thyme UK/USA Garden Thyme UK/USA

THOMPSON & MORGAN

Height: 10–20 cm (4–8 in)
Spread: 23–38 cm (9–15 in)
Hardy, dwarf, spreading evergreen shrub with aromatic leaves. In early to mid-summer it bears clusters of tubular, mauve flowers.

Culinary uses
The leaves, which have a mild, slightly spicy and sweet flavour, are used fresh or dried in stuffings for rich meats, as well as with fish and in *bouquets garnis*. They also add flavour to casseroles. Thyme was a traditional ingredient of jugged hare.

Lemon Thyme

Thymus x *citriodorus* (Lemon Thyme) has lance-shaped to oval, mid-green leaves that emit a distinctive and refreshing, lemon-like scent that is similar to the redolence of Lemon Verbena (see page 29).

Plants grow about 25 cm (10 in) tall and spread to 38 cm (15 in). The leaves are widely used in pot-pourri, as well as being added to desserts.

Raising new plants
Lift and divide congested plants in early or mid-spring; replant young pieces from around the outside and discard old, inner parts. Replant new pieces 23–30 cm (9–12 in) apart. To maintain a supply of leaves from relatively young plants, renewing them is best done every 3–4 years.

Alternatively, in early summer take 5–7.5 cm (2–3 in) long cuttings from sideshoots. Remove the lower leaves and insert them about 2.5 cm (1 in) deep in pots of equal parts moist peat and sharp sand. Place in a cold frame, and when rooted pot the cuttings up into individual pots. Replace in a cold frame and later plant into garden soil.

Looking after plants
Thyme thrives in light, well-drained soil in an open, sunny position. It does well grown in containers, as well as in a herb garden.

Harvesting
Pick off shoots and leaves when needed for using fresh.

For drying, in late summer cut off stems about 15 cm (6 in) long and tie them into bundles of 9–10 shoots. Hang them up to dry in an airy place. Leaves can also be frozen (see page 75).

Mauve flowers

Bushy, spreading, evergreen herb

Spicy, sweet-flavoured leaves

Zingiber officinale

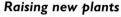

GINGER UK/USA

Canton Ginger USA **Common Ginger** USA **Root Ginger** UK **True Ginger** USA

Height: 60–90 cm (2–3 ft)
Spread: 30–38 cm (12–15 in)

Tropical perennial that can be grown in containers in temperate climates if the roots can be can be given protection in greenhouses from autumn to late spring. Alternatively, grow ginger in a heated greenhouse throughout the year. However, the easiest way to grow Ginger in a cool, temperate climate is to buy fresh roots in spring, put them in pots and harvest the complete crop in autumn.

Plants send up lily-like fronds, sometimes 1 m (3½ ft) high, which develop spikes of yellow, purple-lipped flowers. At the end of the growing season, they will have produced further bulbs that can be used for culinary purposes.

Culinary uses

Grated or finely chopped pieces of root are used to flavour curries, pickles and spiced meat, fish and vegetable dishes. It is also an important flavouring for gingerbread or ginger snaps (cookies). Remember that grated or finely chopped pieces of root have a richer and stronger flavour than powdered roots.

Tropical plant with distinctive, knobbly roots

Raising new plants

The easiest way to do this is to buy a root of ginger in a greengrocer's (vegetable market) or oriental food shop in spring each year. Pot it up into a 20 cm (8 in) wide pot in a well-drained, loam-based compost and thoroughly water. Place in a warm greenhouse.

Looking after plants

Throughout summer, keep the compost moist but not waterlogged. If growing this plant outside in the open garden, choose a warm, wind-sheltered position.

Harvesting

At the end of the growing season, remove the roots; they can be used fresh or dried.

Alternatively, they can be preserved in syrup or vinegar.

Roots were once used to flavour beer

Buying and planting herbs

Much of the success in growing herbs is to buy healthy, correctly labelled, pest-and-disease-free plants that will quickly become established. Most herbs that are bought are growing in containers and mainly sold through garden centres and nurseries. High-street shops, specialist nurseries and mail order provide other opportunities to buy plants. Local horticultural clubs occasionally organize the sale of plants, and this can be a good way to start with herbs.

What should I look for?

PLANTS OR SEEDS?

Getting started with herbs is usually a choice between buying established plants (see below) or packets of seeds (see opposite). There is also the opportunity to take cuttings from established plants (see page 70) or divide herbaceous types (see page 71).

Buying established plants will, of course, produce quick results and is an ideal way to grow long-term herbs such as *Laurus nobilis* (Bay) and *Rosmarinus officinalis* (Rosemary). Many others, such as annual types, can be raised by sowing seeds. It is a relatively inexpensive way to produce herbs, but if you only want a few plants it is often better to buy them from garden centres and nurseries.

Always buy healthy, correctly labelled plants. Check that the compost is moist, but not waterlogged, and that roots are not growing out of the drainage holes in the bottom of the pot.

WHERE TO BUY HERBS: PLANTS

Garden centres

Buying herbs from garden centres is popular and plants can be inspected before you buy them. Advice is often available, too, if you are in doubt about what to buy. They usually sell the most popular herbs.

Specialist nurseries

These nurseries offer a wide range of culinary herbs, as well as those with medicinal qualities. You can visit some nurseries to buy plants; others provide a mail-order service only. They also offer specialist advice.

High-street shops

In spring and summer, these outlets often offer good value-for-money plants, including herbs. Some plants are displayed in shade within the shop, while others are outdoors and in strong sunlight. Check each plant carefully.

By mail order

If you are housebound or have transport difficulties, this is an ideal way to buy plants. Herbs are often advertised in newspapers and magazines. Check the plants immediately after delivery and notify the supplier straight away if there are any problems.

WHERE TO BUY HERBS: SEEDS

Garden centres

Large garden centres sell seeds and these are ideal places to see a range of popular seed-raised culinary herbs. Always buy fresh seeds; check the date on the packet.

Seed catalogues

Ordering through seed catalogues is a popular way to buy culinary herbs, especially if you have transport problems. However, do not wait until the last moment before ordering them.

Specialist nurseries

As well as selling plants, these nurseries usually offer seeds of culinary herbs. They invariably have a wider range of herbs than garden centres do, and are ideal for herb enthusiasts.

GETTING PLANTS HOME

Getting plants home safely is the first stage in successful herb growing. Here are a few pointers to success.

- Preferably, put them in a cool place in your car, but not where children and dogs can get near them.
- Where possible, make a special journey to the nursery so that plants can be taken home quickly before they overheat.
- Where possible, stand plants in boxes that will hold them secure.
- Do not expose plants to draughts.
- Do not leave plants in strong sunlight before they are planted.

PLANTING HERBS

Like other plants, herbs are best planted as soon as possible after getting them home. However, to ensure long-term success it is essential to prepare the plant as well as the soil into which it is to be planted. If these are neglected the plant may not be a success.

I Stand the plant (still in its container) on a flat, well-drained surface and water the compost. If the compost was dry, another watering may be needed. Also, lightly but thoroughly water the planting area.

2 To remove the plant and rootball from the pot, place several fingers over the pot's top and invert it. Tap the rim on a firm surface to loosen the rootball, and then remove the plant.

3 Position the rootball in a hole and check that its top is fractionally below the surface of the surrounding soil. Draw friable soil around the rootball and firm it with your fingers.

Spacing herbs

Like other plants, herbs have a wide range of heights and spreads; these are indicated in the A–Z of culinary herbs (pages 26–65). Therefore, when planting your herbs, position individual plants so that their foliage will later slightly overlap. This will produce a better display than if each plant, when mature, is surrounded by a lot of bare soil, or is too close to its neighbour.

Planting in groups

Where several plants of the same herb are being planted in a group, remember to use odd numbers of plants. A group of three plants in a triangular formation always looks better than two or four in a straight or boxed formation. Groups of herbs in odd numbers are also easily merged in with neighbouring plants.

INITIAL AFTERCARE

After firming soil over each rootball (see above), use a trowel to level the surface; as well as producing an attractive look, it helps to prevent puddles of water appearing after plants are watered. After levelling the surface, gently but thoroughly water the entire area and for about 1 m (3½ ft) around each plant. Later, when the surface soil starts to become dry, again thoroughly water the ground. Whenever the weather is dry, further water may be necessary.

Raising herbs from seeds

What makes seeds germinate?

Seeds germinate when they are given adequate moisture, air and suitable warmth. Most seeds prefer darkness in which to germinate; a few germinate when in light. However, they all need light once young seed leaves appear above the compost or soil's surface. When the essential requirements for germination are present, the seedcoat ruptures and a seed leaf (or leaves) grows up towards the light. At the same time, a root develops.

POPULAR WAY TO RAISE PLANTS

Sowing seeds is the most popular and cheapest way to raise new plants. It is also an ideal way to raise many plants at the same time, and all with similar characteristics. Always buy seeds from a reputable source to ensure they are fresh and of the type you wish to grow.

SAVING SEEDS

If you have seeds left over from one year, it is possible to store them for sowing the next. Seal opened packets with adhesive tape and keep them in a dark, cool place in a closed tin or jar. Check that the date is on the packet. However, seeds of onion-type plants sometimes fail to germinate during the following year; old Parsley seeds are also reluctant to germinate.

Many herbs can be inexpensively raised by sowing seeds.

SOWING SEEDS OUTDOORS

Many herbs (see opposite page) are raised from seeds sown outdoors. Some seeds are sown in their germinating and growing positions, while others are sown in a seedbed and later transferred to where they will grow. Details of the ways herbs are sown and grown are explained in the A–Z of culinary herbs (see pages 26–65).

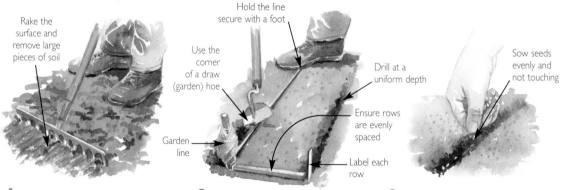

Rake the surface and remove large pieces of soil

Garden line

Hold the line secure with a foot

Use the corner of a draw (garden) hoe

Drill at a uniform depth

Ensure rows are evenly spaced

Label each row

Sow seeds evenly and not touching

1 In winter, dig the soil and remove perennial weeds. A week before sowing, water the seedbed. Allow the surface to become slightly dry, systematically shuffle sideways over the soil to firm it, then rake level.

2 Use a garden (mason's) line to enable a straight drill to be formed by a draw hoe. Standing on the line helps to ensure that the drill is straight. Carefully measure the distances between drills, and label each row.

3 Put some seeds in the palm of one hand and, by gently moving the thumb against the forefinger, enable a few seeds at a time to trickle into the base of the drill. Make sure the seeds are well spaced and not congested.

SOWING SEEDS IN GREENHOUSES

Greenhouses provide assured warmth in which seeds can germinate and young seedlings grow strongly and healthily. The specific temperatures needed by herb seeds to germinate are indicated in the A–Z of culinary herbs (see pages 26–65). Never be tempted to give seeds and young seedlings higher temperatures than recommended – these will not encourage either faster germination or the development of stronger seedlings.

1 Fill a clean seed-tray (flat) with fresh seed compost and use your fingers to firm it, especially at the edges since this is where the compost first becomes dry if watering is neglected.

Compost presser

2 Refill the tray with compost and use a straight piece of wood or a compost presser to level the surface with the tray's (flat's) edges. Then firm the surface to 12 mm (½ in) below the tray's (flat's) rim.

Folded paper

3 Tip a few seeds into the centre of a folded piece of stiff, light-coloured paper. Tap the paper to encourage the seeds to fall evenly on the compost's surface, but not near the edges.

4 Use a flat-based horticultural sieve to cover the seeds with friable compost to 3–4 times their thickness. If such a sieve is not available, use a round-based culinary sieve.

5 Water the compost by standing the seed-tray (flat) in a flat-based bowl shallowly filled with water. When moisture seeps to the surface of the compost, remove and allow excess moisture to drain off.

SUITABLE HERBS

Some herbs are raised from seeds sown outdoors; others need the warmth of a greenhouse. A few herbs can be sown both outdoors and in a greenhouse.

Sowing outdoors

- Angelica (page 31)
- Aniseed (page 55)
- Borage (page 36)
- Caraway (page 38)
- Chervil (page 32)
- Coriander (Cilantro) (page 39)
- Dill (page 30)
- Fennel (page 40)
- Hyssop (page 42)
- Lovage (page 44)
- Marjoram (page 52)
- Parsley (page 54)
- Pot Marigold (page 37)
- Pot Marjoram (page 53)
- Rue (page 58)
- Sorrel (page 57)
- Summer Savory (page 60)
- Sweet Cicely (page 50)
- Tansy (page 63)

Sowing in seed-trays (flats) in greenhouses

- Basil (page 51)
- Bergamot (page 49)
- Marjoram (page 52)
- Pot Marjoram (page 53)
- Sweet Cicely (page 50)

Covering the seeds

Cover the seed-tray (flat) with a sheet of glass and several sheets of newspaper. Turn the glass each day and wipe away condensation; remove both glass and paper after germination.

Raising herbs from cuttings

What is a cutting?

Acutting is any part of a stem, root or leaf that, when separated from a plant and prepared for insertion in well-aerated compost, develops roots. Some cuttings need a warm temperature and an enclosed atmosphere in a greenhouse to encourage rooting, whereas others develop roots when outdoors and inserted in well-drained soil in a sheltered nursery bed. As well as stem cuttings, some culinary herbs have roots that can be used as cuttings.

RAISING PLANTS FROM CUTTINGS

Unlike plants that have been grown from seeds, those raised from cuttings are identical to their parent plant. By taking cuttings, the ensuing plant also has a reserve of energy that helps to give it a good start. However, if the parent plant is infected with a disease or virus, this is usually passed on to the cutting.

CHOICE OF CUTTINGS

Many of the culinary herbs in this book are raised from softwood or half-ripe cuttings (see pages 26–65 for ways to increase specific herbs).

SUITABLE HERBS

Many herbs such as the ones listed below can be increased by taking cuttings from healthy plants.

- Applemint (page 47)
- Bay (page 43)
- Hyssop (page 42)
- Lemon Verbena (page 29)
- Pineapple Mint (page 48)
- Rosemary (page 56)
- Rue (page 58)
- Sage (page 59)
- Southernwood (page 34)
- Spearmint (page 46)
- Tarragon (page 35)
- Thyme (page 64)

TAKING CUTTINGS

Softwood cuttings

Rooting softwood cuttings is a popular and easy way to increase many culinary herbs with soft stems. They need gentle warmth to encourage roots to form. Below is a step-by-step guide to taking and rooting these cuttings.

1 The day before severing shoots, water the 'parent' plant. Dry stems are slow to develop roots. Use a sharp knife or scissors to sever a shoot; cut just above a leaf-joint.

2 Use a sharp knife to sever the shoot fractionally below a leaf-joint to form a cutting 6.5–7.5 cm (2½–3 in) long. Cut off the lower leaves, close to the stem.

3 Fill a pot with equal parts of moist peat and sharp sand and firm to about 12 mm (½ in) below the rim. Use a pencil or dibber (dibble) to insert cuttings into the compost and firm it around their bases. Do not insert cuttings near the pot's sides. Gently but thoroughly water the compost.

Half-ripe cuttings

Also known as semi-hardwood cuttings, these are formed from shoots that are more mature than softwood types. They are taken in mid- and late summer and sometimes include a 'heel' (a piece of older wood still attached to its base). See the A–Z section (pages 26–65) for specific details about these cuttings.

Dividing established herbs

Division is one of the simplest and surest ways to increase plants, especially since there is little risk of divided plants dying before they become established; only a radical loss of moisture in the soil could prevent the regrowth of divided and replanted plants. Young and healthy parts from around the outsides of established clumps are the best parts to replant; the old, central and woody parts should be discarded.

Is dividing plants easy?

AGED AND WOODY

If left alone for many years, herbaceous plants eventually form large clumps that slowly lose their vigour. They have centres full of old, woody stems, with young growth around the edges. The entire clump is best dug up and divided in autumn or late winter. Each clump will yield several new plants.

DIVIDING CLUMPS OF HERBS

Dividing herbs is easy and needs little equipment. For congested clumps growing outdoors, first lift the whole clump; then insert two similarly sized garden forks back to back into the centre, and use them to prise the clump apart. For congested herbs (such as Chives) growing in pots, see below.

1 The day before dividing a congested pot-grown herb, water the compost. To remove the rootball, invert the pot and initially support it. Tap the pot's rim on a firm surface to encourage the rootball to slip out of the pot.

2 If the rootball is especially congested and the central parts woody, use a sharp knife to divide it into several parts. However, the rootball can usually be pulled apart just using your fingers. Discard the old and woody parts.

3 Fill the base of a clean pot with potting compost and position a divided piece of herb in it, with the old soil-mark at its base about 12 mm (½ in) below the rim. Then firm compost around the roots and water the compost.

SUITABLE HERBS

Several herbaceous types of garden herbs, whether growing in pots or outdoors in herb borders, can be divided, as can overgrown clumps of Garlic bulbs.

Herbaceous plants
- Alecost (page 62)
- Applemint (page 47)
- Balm (page 45)
- Bergamot (page 49)
- Chives (page 28)
- Fennel (page 40)
- Lovage (page 44)
- Pineapple Mint (page 48)
- Sorrel (page 57)
- Spearmint (page 46)
- Tansy (page 63)
- Tarragon (page 35)
- Thyme (page 64)

Bulbous plants
- Garlic (page 27)

AFTERCARE

After plants have been lifted and divided, replant the individual pieces as quickly as possible, before their roots become dry. If there is a delay, water the roots and cover them with damp sacking. If you are dividing several different plants, make sure that they do not become mixed up.

DATE AND NAME

Always label and date divided plants. Where the top growth on outdoor herbs has died down, so they cannot be seen, use a cane to indicate their positions.

Harvesting herbs

When should I pick my herbs?

Most herbs are harvested when they are young and fresh, and have their best flavour. The season for harvesting them varies from herb to herb, and this is detailed for each plant in the **A–Z** of culinary herbs (see pages 26–65). To enable the parts of herbs which are used to be readily identified, here are lists of herbs that provide leaves, seeds, stems, roots, bulbs and flowers, which are used to flavour or garnish food and cold, refreshing drinks.

Use a sharp knife to sever leaf stems.

Harvest only the young, healthy leaves; old and damaged ones will have very little eye appeal.

WHEN TO HARVEST HERBS

The time to harvest culinary herbs depends on the part to be used. Plants grown for their stems and leaves are mainly harvested while young and before the flowers appear. Those cultivated for their seeds are harvested when pods ripen and change colour, perhaps first to yellow and then brown. Pick flowers just before they are fully open. Harvest herbs in the morning, after the dew has gone but before the sun becomes excessively hot. Do not harvest them during wet weather.

Take great care not to bruise the flowers.

PARTS OF HERBS FOR CULINARY USE

The technique of harvesting herbs depends on the part which is to be gathered. For detailed information about harvesting each herb, see pages 26–65.

Leaves

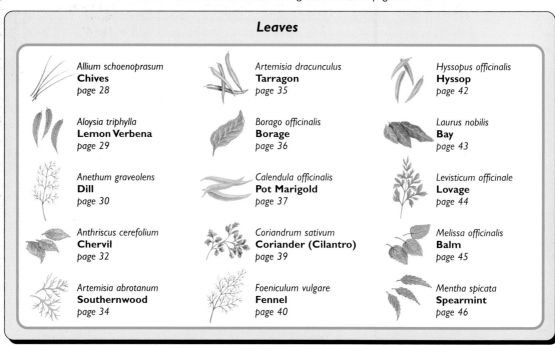

Allium schoenoprasum
Chives
page 28

Aloysia triphylla
Lemon Verbena
page 29

Anethum graveolens
Dill
page 30

Anthriscus cerefolium
Chervil
page 32

Artemisia abrotanum
Southernwood
page 34

Artemisia dracunculus
Tarragon
page 35

Borago officinalis
Borage
page 36

Calendula officinalis
Pot Marigold
page 37

Coriandrum sativum
Coriander (Cilantro)
page 39

Foeniculum vulgare
Fennel
page 40

Hyssopus officinalis
Hyssop
page 42

Laurus nobilis
Bay
page 43

Levisticum officinale
Lovage
page 44

Melissa officinalis
Balm
page 45

Mentha spicata
Spearmint
page 46

PARTS OF HERBS FOR CULINARY USE (CONTINUED)

Leaves (continued)

Mentha suaveolens
Applemint
page 47

Mentha suaveolens
'Variegata'
Pineapple Mint
page 48

Monarda didyma
Bergamot
page 49

Myrrhis odorata
Sweet Cicely
page 50

Ocimum basilicum
Basil
page 51

Origanum majorana
Marjoram
page 52

Origanum onites
Pot Marjoram
page 53

Petroselinum crispum
Parsley
page 54

Rosmarinus officinalis
Rosemary
page 56

Rumex scutatus
Sorrel
page 57

Ruta graveolens
Rue
page 58

Salvia officinalis
Sage
page 59

Satureja hortensis
Summer Savory
page 60

Satureja montana
Winter Savory
page 61

Tanacetum balsamita
Alecost
page 62

Tanacetum vulgare
Tansy
page 63

Thymus vulgaris
Thyme
page 64

Seeds

Anethum graveolens
Dill
page 30

Carum carvi
Caraway
page 38

Coriandrum sativum
Coriander
page 39

Foeniculum vulgare
Fennel
page 40

Levisticum officinale
Lovage
page 44

Myrrhis odorata
Sweet Cicely
page 50

Pimpinella anisum
Aniseed
page 55

Stems

Angelica archangelica
Angelica
page 31

Levisticum officinale
Lovage
page 44

Roots

Armoracia rusticana
Horseradish
page 33

Glycyrrhiza glabra
Liquorice
page 41

Zingiber officinale
Ginger
page 65

Bulbs

Allium sativum
Garlic
page 27

Flowers

Borago officinalis
Borage
page 36

Calendula officinalis
Pot Marigold
page 37

Monarda didyma
Bergamot
page 49

Drying and freezing herbs

*Do herbs
keep for
very long?*

Most herbs are best used when freshly harvested, and many of those grown for their leaves can be kept for a limited time in individual dry, airtight containers. There is also the possibility of drying or freezing them, however. Drying herbs in well-ventilated, airy and fairly warm places is a traditional way to preserve them, and has been undertaken for many centuries, but freezing herbs, either whole or chopped, is relatively new.

STORING DRIED HERBS IN JARS

When storing herbs in airtight containers, ensure that they are put in dark, cool cupboards. Avoid shelves positioned over ovens, as the temperature will fluctuate. Also, use cupboards away from steamy cookers. If properly dried and stored, herbs will retain their flavour for about a year. Label and date the container. Remember that flavours in dried herbs are more concentrated than when fresh and therefore need to be used sparingly; often only about half the normal amount.

FLAVOURING STEWS

Stews, as well as soups and casseroles, can be easily flavoured by using frozen cubes of herbs (see page 75). Simply add them into a dish, without thawing, before cooking. Slightly crumbling the cube will speed up thawing.

Suitable herbs

The decision to use herbs fresh, dried or frozen depends on the time of year and the nature of the herb. In the A–Z of culinary herbs (see pages 26–65) there are suggestions about harvesting.

Best fresh

All herbs are best used when freshly picked, but there are several months of the year when this is impossible for most herbs. Evergreen herbs such as *Rosmarinus officinalis* (Rosemary) and *Laurus nobilis* (Bay), as well as perennial types that are overwintered indoors in pots, are available throughout the year, but from autumn to spring it is usually necessary to rely on herbs that have been dried or frozen.

Good for drying

Where herbs are grown for their leaves and stems, these parts should be gathered while young and healthy and, preferably, before the plant flowers. Large leaves, such as those of *Salvia officinalis* (Sage), can be removed from their stems before drying, but small ones are best left on their stems. Thoroughly check the leaves to ensure they have not been damaged by pests and diseases.

Ideal for freezing

This is an ideal way to preserve some culinary herbs, especially those with tender leaves that are unsuitable for drying. Herbs often frozen include Basil, Chervil, Parsley, Chives and Mint. The herbs retain their flavour, although on thawing are limp and are best used for flavouring food rather than as garnishes. These herbs are best used within six months of being frozen.

Bunches of herbs when drying are highly decorative and introduce a rustic ambience to drying areas.

HOW TO DRY HERBS

There are two main ways to dry herbs – in the air or by placing in a slightly warmed oven. The easiest and best way is by exposing severed parts to air, but both techniques are initially the same.

BLANCHING HERBS

Blanching herbs (see Glossary) prior to drying them is often recommended, but is not essential. However, it helps leaves to retain their colours.

← Dry large leaves by spacing them on wire trays. Place in a warm place (such as an airing cupboard or a warming drawer in an oven) for a day or two. Turn the leaves every day to ensure even drying.

↑ Small-leaved or feathery herbs are best dried by tying them in bunches and hanging them upside down in a warm, airy place. Avoid humid kitchens. Drying takes 5–10 days.

HOW TO DRY SEEDHEADS

Several herbs, such as Dill, Fennel and Coriander, are grown for their seeds, which can be used to add distinctive flavours to food. Drying the seedheads is easy and requires little in the way of equipment.

← To harvest seeds, pick the seedheads when fully ripe, tie their stems in bunches and suspend in a warm, airy place until dry. Enclose them in a paper or muslin (cheesecloth) bag to capture all the seeds.

← When the seedheads are completely dry, you can remove the seeds from the surrounding material. Use a culinary sieve to separate the seeds, then store them in a dry, airtight jar in a dark, cool cupboard.

HOW TO FREEZE HERBS

There are two ways in which herbs can be frozen: freezing whole and freezing in water. With both methods, it is essential to select young, healthy herbs that have not been damaged by pests or diseases.

← Freezing herbs whole involves picking young leaves or shoots and packing them in airtight plastic bags to prevent aromas spreading. Place these in rigid containers to protect them from being squashed; place in a freezer.

← Freezing in water involves washing and chopping leaves, placing them in ice-cube trays and topping up with water. Put them in a freezer compartment and add the cubes directly to food before or during cooking.

Pests and diseases

Are herbs susceptible?

Like all other plants, especially those with flowers and soft stems, herbs are likely at some time to be attacked by pests and diseases. Some pests chew roots, as well as stems, leaves and flowers. Diseases are likely to cause damage to soft parts of herbs, including young and vulnerable seedlings. Some pests are general to many plants; these include caterpillars, greenfly (aphids), millipedes, slugs and snails.

Greenfly (aphids)

Greenfly suck sap, causing mottling and distortion. They tend to congregate under leaves and around leaf-joints and buds, as well as in soft flowers. Aphids also transmit viruses from plant to plant, causing further devastation. As soon as greenfly are seen, use a spray suitable for edible crops.

Cockchafer grubs

Cockchafer grubs live in garden soil and graze on the roots of plants, causing them to wilt and, often, die. The grubs pupate and beetles appear. Where possible, pick off and destroy beetles, as well as the grubs when the soil is being dug. Dig new herb gardens deeply in winter to expose the grubs and to remove them.

Caterpillars

Caterpillars chew soft stems and leaves, rapidly decimating them until, if left, the plant becomes a skeleton of its former self. Pick off caterpillars and spray with an insecticide for use on food crops. Also clear away and burn all rubbish during the winter to restrict their spread and numbers.

Cutworms

Cutworms are the larvae of certain moths. They chew seedlings and plants at ground level, causing them to collapse and giving the appearance of being cut down. When preparing a new herb bed, thoroughly dig the soil and pick out and destroy the larvae. Also hoe around plants throughout summer.

Damping off

Damping off is mainly a disease of young seedlings in greenhouses. It is exacerbated by badly drained compost and high humidity. Seedlings appear to collapse at compost level, due to the withering of the stem at that point. Use well-drained compost, water it carefully to prevent waterlogging, and avoid high humidity.

Earwigs

Earwigs are pernicious and omnipresent pests. They clamber into plants, eating soft stems, leaves and flowers. Pick them off and destroy. Also, trap them in pots filled with straw and inverted on bamboo canes. Alternatively, spray or dust with a pesticide suitable for use on edible crops.

Flea beetles

Flea beetles chew roundish holes in seedlings and especially in young leaves. They become unsightly and ineffective. Flea beetles are especially active during sunny days in late spring. Carefully spray with an insecticide suitable for food crops. Also keep the soil hoed and free from rubbish.

Millipedes

Millipedes have two pairs of legs on each body segment and are slower-moving than centipedes. They chew all parts of plants, from young roots, tubers, bulbs and stems to seedlings. Dust with an insecticide and remove all rubbish from around plants. Hoeing also helps to ensure they cannot hide in surface soil.

Grey mould (botrytis)

Grey mould (botrytis) is a destructive fungal disease that enters plants through cuts and wounds. It appears as a fluffy mould on leaves, stems and flowers, especially where damp and airless conditions prevail. Avoid congesting plants, and remove all infected tissue, to reduce the risk of the disease spreading.

Snails

Snails, like slugs, are pests of the night and especially damaging during warm, wet weather. They chew and tear leaves and stems. Pick off and destroy them as soon as they are seen. Also use baits in the same way as for slugs. After there has been a shower of rain, snails often appear in large numbers.

Weevils

Weevils are beetle-like and they are characterized by having long, divided snouts. Their larvae are legless grubs, and both adult beetles and larvae feed on roots, stems and leaves. They quickly decimate plants, making them unsightly. Regularly dust or spray with an insecticide suitable for edible crops.

Wireworms

Wireworms are the larvae of click beetles, which eat roots, stems, bulbs and tubers. They are prevalent in newly prepared land, especially former grassland. Eradicating weeds from around plants helps to prevent infestations, as do regular hoeing and dusting the soil with insecticides.

Woodlice

Woodlice are hard-coated pests, living in damp and dark places. They come out at night and feed on stems, roots and leaves. Herbs growing near to old buildings are especially at risk as woodlice lurk in and around old brickwork. Remove all rubbish from the area and dust the soil with a pesticide.

Mint rust

Mint rust is a pernicious disease and one that is difficult to eradicate without digging up and burning seriously infected plants. It first appears in spring, causing orange, later black, pustule-like spores on stems. The remedy is always to buy healthy plants and to plant them in clean, fresh soil.

Slugs

Slugs are destructive and soon decimate plants. They are especially troublesome during wet and warm weather, when they chew all parts of plants. They mainly feed at night and therefore are not always seen. Use slug baits or remove and destroy them. Ensure that the baits are not accessible to family pets and wildlife.

USING GARDEN CHEMICALS

When using a chemical, always adhere to the manufacturer's instructions and thoroughly wash all equipment after use. Also check that the chemical is suitable for food crops, and that the recommended period between spraying and harvesting is observed.

SAFETY FIRST

- Store garden chemicals away from children and animals - and make sure the bottle or package is labelled.
- Do not mix chemicals, unless you are specifically instructed to do so.
- If you have an accident, seek medical advice immediately – and take along the chemical and its packaging.

Glossary

Annual A plant that grows from seed, flowers and dies within the same year. Several herbs, such as Borage and Dill, are annuals. Additionally, a few herbs, such as Parsley, are hardy biennials but invariably grown as annuals. See also Hardy annuals and Half-hardy annuals.

Apothecary A person who prepares and sells drugs and medicines. It is a term better known in earlier centuries; today, such a person would be a pharmacist.

Biennial A plant that grows from seed, making initial growth one year and flowering during the following one; then dying.

Blanching Sometimes used to help herbs retain their colour prior to drying, it involves dipping them in boiling water for a few seconds. Blanching is said to stop enzyme activity.

Bolting Describes a plant that prematurely develops seeds, rather than continuing normal growth. Usually caused by drought, hot weather or exceptionally poor soil.

Bouquet garni (pl. *bouquets garnis*) A bunch of herbs, tied together or wrapped in cheesecloth, used to season food, including soups, stews and sauces.

Cartwheel herb garden An arrangement of herbs, as if planted between the spokes of a cartwheel. If a wheel is not available, it can be simulated by stones to form the rim, spokes and hub.

Clove A segment of a garlic bulb.

Compost The mixture in which cuttings are inserted, seeds are sown and plants replanted or potted. Can also refer to decomposed vegetative material, which is better known as garden compost.

Culinary Relating to cooking and the kitchen.

Cultivar A plant produced in cultivation and indicating a cultivated variety. Earlier, all variations, whether produced naturally in the wild or in cultivation, were known as 'varieties'. As the term 'variety' has been known to gardeners for many decades, it is still frequently used.

Cutting A severed part of a plant that is encouraged to form roots as a method of vegetative propagation.

Deciduous A plant that loses its leaves at the beginning of its dormant season. This usually applies to woody plants such as trees, shrubs and some climbers. A few conifers are deciduous.

Dibber (dibble) Pencil-like rod with a rounded end. Used to transfer seedlings to wider spacings in seed-trays and to insert cuttings into compost in pots and seed-trays. Larger and thicker dibbers are used to plant vegetables such as leeks, cabbages and cauliflowers.

Division A vegetative method of propagation, involving dividing roots. It is often performed on herbaceous plants.

Edible landscaping A North American term for growing herbs, vegetables and fruit together with a medley of flowers in an informal style.

Essential oil A volatile oil, usually having the characteristic odour of the plant from which it is derived, and used to make perfumes and flavourings.

Evergreen Describes a plant that continuously sheds and grows new leaves throughout the year and therefore at any one time appears to have a complete array of leaves and to be 'ever green'. Many trees, shrubs and conifers are evergreen.

Fines herbes A French term for finely chopped herbs. They are used fresh or dried, as seasonings and to flavour sauces.

Garnish To use herbs, either whole or chopped, to enhance the appearance of food and to add further flavours.

Germination The process that occurs within a seed when given adequate moisture, air and warmth. The seedcoat ruptures and a seed leaf (or leaves) grows up and towards the light. At the same time, a root develops. However, to most gardeners, germination is when they see seed leaves appearing through the surface of compost or soil.

Half-hardy annuals Plants sown in gentle warmth early in the year and later planted outdoors when the weather improves.

Harden off To acclimatize plants to outdoor conditions. Usually applies to plants raised in greenhouses in late winter and early spring, which need gently and slowly to be accustomed to lower temperatures outdoors, before being planted.

Hardy Describes a plant that in temperate climates is able to be left outside during winter.

Hardy annual A plant sown directly into its growing and flowering position outdoors. The seed germinates, and the plant grows and produces flowers within the same year. The plant then dies.

Heel cutting A method of increasing woody plants, including some herbs. Part of an older shoot is left attached to the base of each cutting.

Herbaceous Describes a plant that dies down to soil level in autumn or early winter and develops fresh shoots in spring. Balm is an example of a herbaceous herb.

Herbal A book containing names and descriptions of herbs, their uses and properties.

Herbal tea An infusion of one or more herbs. Usually forms a refreshing or medicinal drink.

Medicinal herbs Those herbs that have curative and healing powers, derived from roots, stems, leaves and flowers.

Nosegay An early term for a bunch of fragrant, attractive flowers, but a word still occasionally used. Also known as a posy.

Physic(k) garden A garden or area primarily devoted to growing medicinal plants.

Pomander A mixture of aromatic substances in an apple-shaped container. Formerly regarded as protection against infection, nowadays it is used to perfume rooms.

Posy (pl. posies) A small bunch of flowers, usually fragrant. A more recent term for nosegay.

Potage gardening Growing herbs, vegetables and fruit together with a medley of flowers in an informal style.

Pot-pourri (pl. pot-pourris) A mixture of fragrant petals and spices kept in a jar and used to scent the air.

Pricking off The initial moving of seedlings from where they were sown in pots or seed-trays to wider spacings in other seed-trays or pots.

Propagators Enclosed, plastic- or glass-covered units in which seeds are encouraged to germinate and cuttings to root. Some are heated.

Root cutting Method of increasing certain plants by cutting up roots and inserting them either vertically or horizontally in well-aerated compost in pots or seed-trays.

Sauce tartare See Tartare sauce.

Seed-tray (flat) Flat-based tray in which seeds are sown and seedlings grown. Known in North America as a 'flat'.

Self-sown seedlings Seedlings that occur naturally around some plants.

Synonym An alternative botanical name for a plant.

Tartare sauce Also known as *Sauce tartare* and tartar sauce. A sauce formed of mayonnaise mixed with chopped onions, chives, pickles and capers, and served as a sauce with fish.

Thinning Removing congested seedlings to leave healthy ones that then have more space in which to develop and grow strongly.

Transplanting Moving young plants from a nursery bed to the position in which they will grow and mature. The term is also used when established plants are moved.

Variety See Cultivar.

Index

Acknowledgments

AG&G Books would like to thank **Richo Cech** of **Horizon Herbs, LLC** for supplying photographs of their herbs. Horizon Herbs is a family-run farm in Southern Oregon, USA that grows over 700 medicinal plant species. They focus on seed work and sell nursery stock. Contact Horizon Herbs, PO Box 69, 3350 Cedar Flat Road, Williams, OR 97544, telephone (541) 8466704, www.horizonherbs.com for a free catalogue. Richo Cech is the author of *Making Plant Medicine* (2000) and *Growing At-Risk Medicinal Herbs* (2002). AG&G Books would also like to thank **Thompson & Morgan**, Quality Seedsmen Since 1855, *brings the finest quality flower and vegetable seed and flower plant varieties to the home gardener,* Thompson & Morgan (UK) Ltd, Poplar Lane, Ipswich, Suffolk, IP8 3BU and the RHS Gardens at Hyde Hall, Rettendon, Chelmsford, Essex, England and at Wisley, Woking, Surrey, England. Photographs: AG&G Books (pages 2, 3, 8, 12, 14, 15, 16, 18TL, 22TL, BL and BR, 24, 27, 28, 29, 30, 31, 32, 34, 37, 40, 43, 44, 45, 48, 52, 60, 63, 65, 66, 68 and 74), Garden Matters (cover front and pages 22BR, 55 and 57), Horizon Herbs (pages 22BORAGO OFFICINALIS and SALVIA OFFICINALIS, 35, 36, 41, 42, 46, 50, 58, 59, 61, 62 and 72), Peter McHoy (pages 18C, 22TR and BR, 33, 38 and 39) and Thompson & Morgan (pages 18, 22TR, 51, 54, 56 and 64).